My Shangri-La

Sally Swope

Sasha Press
San Francisco, CA
www.sashapress.com

Published by Sasha Press
San Francisco
www.sashapress.com

ISBN-13: 978-0-9788862-8-8
Printed in the United States of America

To Rick Lawton

for his unwavering support

The big question is whether you are going to say a hearty yes to your adventure.

Joseph Campbell
A Hero's Journey

My Shangri-La

Contents

Introduction

You wouldn't think that I'd have anything to do with Asia. I grew up 2,400 miles from the West Coast in Ohio and I can't think how far from Asia. One summer night I stayed up late and by chance I tuned into a movie about a fantastic place called Shangri-La. Was Shangri-La real or imaginary I wondered?

I felt a sense of awe that there might be a place like this paradise somewhere in Asia. My memoir begins with this story and includes my adventures traveling in Asia in the late 1980s and early 1990s when few Americans traveled there and even fewer single women ventured there on their own.

I left home on a vacation to Bangkok in 1985 and in the next eight years traveled there frequently. I found the most interesting stories were about local cultural festivals, sacred places, and environmental wonders. Chance and good luck influenced all of my trips and along the way I learned a lot about the people I encountered, their religious traditions and strong family ties.

Shangri-La and Asia must have stayed in the back of my mind, because I focused on Asian studies in graduate school. My mentor designed a curriculum of small classes and independent studies with curators at the Cleveland Museum of Art. I studied the arts, culture, and history of Japan, China and India. And I studied conversational Japanese. I knew a lot about Asia and hoped I'd have the opportunity to visit someday. Six months after I arrived in San Francisco in 1979, my first article on Japanese paintings at the Asian Art Museum was published in *Artweek*.

Two years later in my mid-30s, I got to Asia when my husband took me on a honeymoon to Japan. By that time I was an established freelance writer. Later my curiosity, drive and work as a journalist, travel writer, and photographer enabled me to visit Asia on my own. It took a lot of planning and skill because each trip was different. Also, I didn't have the funds to travel and I was working full-time.

For my trips, I worked with magazine editors and cultural officers at consulates, travel agents, and local tourism experts.

And, of course, I had to convince my supervisors that I needed the time off. Most of the time, I was out of work for a month which was a financial strain. My first travel piece paid $150, but during that month, I had been to Sumatra, Java, and Bali.

Several people influenced my call to adventure. I knew travel writers in the National Writers Union who knew how to approach editors and gain press trips. One of these writers, Rebecca Bruns, shared how she gained assistance from the Mexican Tourism Office and developed a relationship with them.

An artist, Edie Hamlin, gave me inspiration from the way she lived. She told me of leaving New York after the stock market crashed, driving cross country with a friend and arriving in San Francisco in time to gain a mural commission at Coit Tower. Later one of her huge murals hung in the International Wing of the San Francisco International Airport. Edie was not only an inspiration, but also a good friend.

Another influence was Eve Arnold, a photojournalist for *The Sunday Times* of London. I interviewed her when she was promoting her new book, *In China*. With the opportunity to visit China, she got a three-week visa to Mongolia and was the first photographer to show the world this secluded place. She encouraged me to travel to Asia and take photos.

I quickly discovered that it was easy meeting strangers and finding out about them and their country. I wrote about what interested me and the unexpected things that happened along the way. What made these trips so special was my intention to be there.

I gained more emotional intelligence and greater trust of my intuition and as result became a better risk-taker. Twenty-five years after these exciting adventures, I'm still fascinated with Asia's cultures, politics, and its influence on the world.

Sally Swope
San Francisco, 2014

Countries visited in Asia

Life Before Asia

My first travel fantasies

My first fantasy to see Asia began by watching a movie, *Lost Horizon*, late one summer night on TV when my sisters and parents were in bed. The film told a fantastic story of a lost paradise like nowhere else on earth. This magical place was hidden in the Himalayas and the people there lived to be hundreds of years old. They had a kind of wisdom that made them content and happy. Even at age eight, I knew this place wasn't real but it represented the richness that Asia holds for a new traveler.

Asia entered my dreams at age eight

This fantasy place was called Shangri-La, a place first mentioned in the 1933 popular mass-produced paperback novel, *Lost Horizon,* by James Hilton. The novel was so popular that "Shangri-La" soon became a household word. President Franklin Roosevelt called Camp David Shangri-La.

Hilton drew his inspiration from a travelogue of two French priests who traveled between Beijing and Lhasa in 1844-46. Many scholars speculate that Shangri-La is Shambhala, a mythical kingdom in Tibetan Buddhist tradition, which was sought by Eastern and Western explorers. Four years after the novel *Lost Horizon* was published, Frank Capra made it into a film starring

Ronald Coleman as Robert Conway and Jane Wyatt as Sondra. In the film, Conway, an English diplomat, rescues four people caught in China's civil war.

The plane flying them to London and safety crashes in the Himalayas, and a guide rescues them from certain death and takes them to Shangri-La, a fantastic warm valley where people live happily, invigorated by their friends and work.

Conway is trying to make sense of all the mysteries of Shangri-La when he is summoned to a meeting with the High Lama, who tells him he has been chosen to become the next leader of the community. After this pronouncement, the High Lama suddenly dies. Conway decides not to take on this leadership role and leaves the utopia. Many years later he is desperate to return but he can't find Shangri-La.

My hometown had the appearance of a Shangri-La. The town came together each October to celebrate the farmers and the bounty of their harvest. Circleville was known state-wide for its Pumpkin Show which included marching bands, parades with floats, scary rides, pumpkin taffy, and people looking at hundreds of pumpkins on display. The Pumpkin Show of my youth was a charming small town tradition. I remember that when I was six my twin sister and I rode on the front of a family friend's convertible sports car in the Pumpkin Show Parade, waving to the crowds, hoping to be chosen as Little Miss Pumpkin Show.

Despite enjoying the security of small-town America in the fifties, I fantasized about leaving. My home life was chaotic and unstable. My parents played favorites and often were fighting behind closed doors. Me and my sisters wanted to return to the comfortable and calm life we had grown up with. Despite their final try to reunite, my parents soon divorced. My life soon turned upside down. We moved to a ritzy suburb of Columbus and my class of 60 turned into a class of 600. We rarely saw my dad, and my mom went to graduate school and began working full time. I desperately wanted to leave home and escape to a far-off Shangri-La.

Me and my twin sister in the Pumpkin Show Parade

Biking in Central Europe

At the age of 17, I won an all-expense-paid, six-week bike trip to Europe for my 100-word essay about why I wanted to be a young ambassador. I could barely contain my excitement. I practiced riding long distances on the flat country roads of Pickaway County, Ohio, where corn and soybeans were farmed outside of Circleville.

The contest was funded as a public relations stunt by the Wrangler Blue Jeans Company, and American Youth Hostels organized the itinerary. There were 100 winners and my group of ten traveled through England, Belgium, Southern Germany, France, and Switzerland by train, boat, and bicycle.

The *Columbus Dispatch* even wrote an article about me on July 10, 1967, with the headline, "Girl Wins Trip Abroad with Essay on People." The story focused on my fantasy to be a young ambassador.

On my bicycle trip to Europe, I'm second from left

This bike trip happened in an unexpected way. In my junior year, I attended a large high school with 600 students in my class. Almost all of my school's 1,800 students went to college. I was picked to lead the student exchange club, American Field Service, for both my junior and senior years of high school.

During that time, the club hosted students from Saigon, Tokyo, Johannesburg, and Santiago. With a group of friends, I helped the new students feel welcome but I was disappointed that there was a shortage of home stays abroad, which meant I wouldn't go abroad after my senior year.

This was the first time synchronicity emerged in my life. My mom was shopping in a department store and saw a poster about a free trip to Europe by a rack of Wrangler blue jeans. From a small pad of forms, she tore off an application with the rules of the contest that would send students age 17 to 23 to Europe for free. That night I condensed my essay for the AFS home stay in a foreign country into 100 carefully chosen words and sent it in the next day.

In less than a month, I was on my way to London's Carnaby Street, where I promptly bought a pair of yellow patent-leather sandals—the most exciting purchase in my life at that time. I found it comfortable to ride my bike in a mini-dress. We had to wear Wrangler's clothes but that was the only expectation.

My two saddlebags full of everything I needed weighed about 35 pounds. Riding down mountains fast was harder than going up because it was so easy to flip the bike. We rode approximately 1,200 miles over the summer.

The trip began in New York; we flew to London and took the ferry from Dover to Ostend, Belgium. At our first stop in Bruges, Netherlands, a teenager named Andre rode past us on his bike and then came back to ask if we needed directions. He wanted to meet Americans as much as we wanted to meet some locals. Before we left, Andre said he'd meet me in Paris. The day after we arrived in fabulous Paris, a city I dreamed of visiting, he met me as promised.

Andre was tall and muscular, about my age, spoke four languages, and flirted with me a lot. My hormones were revved up as he turned me on. We took the train to Versailles and walked through the maze of gardens, and room after room of paintings and ornate gold-leaf mirrors.

9

With Bob, one of the bikers in my group

One night we were out at 1:30 a.m. strolling around the Night Market in Paris. We had French onion soup in a café called Le Chien Qui Fume (The Dog That Smokes). Several butchers with blood-stained aprons also ate in the small space.

I was glad my best friend, Karen, had given me a small yellow notebook to capture my first impressions. And my dad gave me a Canon camera before I left. Looking through the viewer helped me to see composition and focus on whatever caught my attention. This bike trip expanded my confidence and opened my view of the world exponentially. My senior year of high school I joined the world events club and considered going to college to be an ambassador.

Communing in Haight Ashbury

Not all of my time was spent reading and dreaming about Asia. In retrospect, I was also adventurous, sometimes to a fault. On my summer break after my junior year at Kirkland College near Utica, New York, I was back home in Ohio and found a job waitressing with a friendly, outgoing girl named Susie. She liked to say she had gypsy blood; her black straight hair hung to her waist and she had a huge smile and laughed a lot to punctuate her sentences.

Susie and I believed our talents weren't developed to their full potential by serving dinners and drinks. We felt trapped and we asked ourselves, what are we going to do with a liberal arts education? We deferred answering that questions and began fantasizing about traveling and seeing the rest of the country. What was it like on the West Coast? Could we really hitch to San Francisco? Did we have the courage to try?

Then we began to think about the idea of visiting Susie's friend in San Francisco. Neither of us had hitched. What if we didn't make it home? Or were kidnapped? What would I do if I was really scared or ran out of money?

We might end up stranded but I decided I wasn't going to call home and ask for money. This was my first trip and I wanted to do it without my parents' help. I took the leap on the biggest adventure of my life and was determined to make it home safely—I said this many times to myself.

I saw the trip as a kind of initiation rite: traveling to the West Coast, and facing unknown danger and hardship. I was reading *The Teachings of Don Juan* and felt empowered at the idea of a shaman who could change into an animal or some other form through magic rituals and peyote. It colored my thinking.

Despite our many apprehensions about hitching and going so far from home on our excursion, we took off and a few days later landed in the Panhandle, a neighborhood in San Francisco, next to Golden Gate Park and the Haight Ashbury.

When we arrived, almost no one believed it took us only four days to get to San Francisco and we had only spent ten dollars. Each driver asked if our parents knew where we were. Times were different then and many young people hitched. One ride in a white VW bus took us from Colorado with Pike's Peak in the distance, and dropped us off at the Victorian home in the Panhandle where Susie's friend lived.

San Francisco just after the Summer of Love

When we arrived, the morning fog was lifting over the city and we saw the skyline emerge.

Susie and I met her friends at their communal flat as one of the women was running out the door for her temp job downtown. Another guy left on his bike and said he'd be back in the afternoon for the weekly food distribution in their driveway. They gave away food to people who needed it.

The front room walls were covered with large black and white photos of women and I asked Susie's friend who they were. She said they were transvestites in a group called the Coquettes that had a late-night show at The Palace Theater in North Beach. The photos were tame compared to the freaky show of raunchy sexual acts on stage we saw a few nights later. It left me wondering if I'd like living there.

We got into the scene: we were young, carefree, and naïve. A few nights later, we went to a drive-in movie theater to see *What Ever Happened to Baby Jane*. Everyone dropped acid at the drive-in so I tried it too. The movie seemed to disappear as the light show and weird images floated in my mind. I saw my feet coming out of my mouth like I was turning inside out. The acid was way too strong for me and I decided I wouldn't take any more. My awareness of the world was changing.

After that trip I wasn't the same kid from Ohio. When I got home, my mom was furious. But the trip had excited me and I secretly knew I'd continue my adventures.

Kerum Shalom in the Sinai

A month after I returned to Ohio from San Francisco, I began to think about an alternative to college. I still had a wanderlust to see more of the world. Could I hitch in a foreign country? I began to think I'd try it.

My Mom had a good friend who was Jewish and she described life on a kibbutz. It seemed like a farm and a commune and this combination appealed to me. I still had enough money for airfare and I knew it cost almost nothing to live there!

Before I left, I remember my parents saying, "Rethink your plans and don't go. It's a ridiculous fantasy."

At the Mosque of Omar, Jerusalem

I felt bravado like I'd never known. I closed my eyes, came to a place I trusted In myself and felt empowered to experience a completely new kind of life. I wanted more than my college days of sitting at a desk taking notes on Renaissance painting.

In Tel Aviv, I was assigned to a tiny kibbutz in the Negev, Kerum Shalom, thirty miles south of Beer'shiva close to the border of what later became known as the Gaza Strip. I was soon picking and pruning red carnations for sale in Tel Aviv and Munich. The kibbutz was an outpost, a way to claim more land for Israel. It was a dangerous area and the young men who kept watch at night were at risk of being killed by Arabs.

Bonding with the Israelis was easy—we were equally crazy about the Beatles and all twenty of us were about the same age. Unlike most kibbutim, there were no kids or Hebrew classes. I was glad two guys about my age from Philly were there too. They shared Mao's radical ideas from his famous little red book.

One day a group of us from the kibbutz went swimming in the Mediterranean and we stopped on the way to meet a friendly family. The herdsman introduced his sons and goats, and then pointed to the door of his small home to show us his wife and daughter peering out at us. Many times, I saw women treated as second-class citizens with less value than animals. I was furious at this culture where the norm for women was to be subservient.

After a couple of months, I was homesick and said my good-byes before leaving the desert. I was on my way back to Ohio to finish college.

From shore to shining shore

I decided to finish college at Ohio State University where I had enough credits to graduate in a year. I took a class with three graduate students that culminated in an exhibit of Oceanic art at the Columbus Museum of Art. I catalogued and displayed exotic masks and shields with phallic images that came from the Sepik River area. As part of this course I saw Margaret Mead's films on several tribes in New Guinea and a trance dance in Bali, which she filmed in the 1930s.

After that experience, I wanted to curate exhibits and headed to graduate school at Case Western Reserve University in Cleveland, Ohio. I felt an immediate connection to Case Western because my dad studied there before he went to medical school in New York on the GI bill.

I studied with the curators at the Cleveland Museum. Two of my favorite pieces were rare Japanese folding screens more than 400 years old. The two six-panel screens were stunning and conveyed the season of springtime with a gray-blue heron by a pond with pale pink peonies and big craggy rocks with ax-cut strokes. The ax-cut strokes were like a signature by a well-known painter Sesshu Toyo (1420-1506).

After graduating, I moved to Washington, D.C. and was active in the Women's Art Center where I met several new friends. I was part of a small group that went to the White House Oval Office where President Carter gave awards to several outstanding artists like Louise Nevelson and Selma Burke.

President Carter walked around his spacious office with a huge smile showing us gifts from Deng Xiaoping, the Vice Premier of the People's Republic of China. He was the first Chinese leader to visit since the founding of the PRC in 1949. He gave President Carter lavish gifts, including some of the finest Chinese art—several bronze vessels with some of the first dragon images.

For a year I worked in the Smithsonian's National Associates Program, which brought people from around the country to explore Washington. I learned a lot about the city quickly. During this time, I lived in a three-story Victorian house called Hard Art because the first floor was used as a gallery. I took dance classes several times a week at the Dance Exchange across the alley.

Even though Washington had a lot going for it, I decided to move to San Francisco where I had friends and many good memories. I knew I'd like it there. I left my job on a leap of faith and imagination to see myself happy and challenged, living in one of the most beautiful cities in the world.

After flying to San Francisco, I was lucky to find work in a public relations agency that paid much better than working in the arts. In one week, I found a job and joined a group in an Edwardian house in the Haight with a hot tub in the back yard.

Six months after I arrived in San Francisco, I saw an amazing exhibit of Japanese paintings at the Asian Art Museum, which has one of the best collections of Asian art in the country. I was so moved by these paintings, which were influenced by Zen beliefs, that I just wrote a review. I'd never done anything like that before. It was an expression of joy!

My review was published as a cover story in *Artweek*, the local weekly newspaper that was an arbiter of good taste and named innovative contemporary artists. I was excited to see my byline in this prestigious local art publication. My writing career started with this article.

The Japanese paintings were done at the time of the samurai, in the 16th century in Kyoto during the Muromachi Period. These paintings were the opposite of the contemporary aesthetic. The ancient Japanese painters showed variations on timeless themes that the artists reworked with their own interpretations.

After that review, the publisher of *Artweek* took most of my reviews of Asian art. The Bay Area had some of the best Asian art in the world. I was in the right place at the right time and my writing took off.

During the next three years in San Francisco, I worked for several public relations agencies full-time. I enjoyed meeting friends, going to movies, hiking, meditating at the Zen Center, and writing more articles.

When I was 32, I met a fascinating man by answering a classified ad in the *San Francisco Bay Guardian*. I was excited to meet a Chinese psychiatrist since I had just finished reading Erica Jong's book, *Fear of Flying*. Like the main character, I had many sexual fantasies as a liberated women. As she was ambivalent about leaving her psychoanalyst husband, I was ambivalent about starting a relationship with a Chinese psychiatrist.

Francis was cute, smart, and fun to be with. He managed an inpatient ward of people with psychiatric problems at San Francisco General Hospital. He was into the transpersonal spiritual realm of psychology which interested me also. We met friends for dinner and went to the opening of the new Davies Symphony Hall. We enjoyed many rafting trips in California and Nevada.

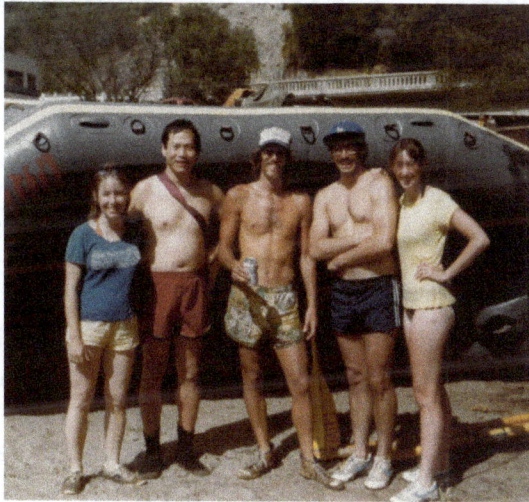

Rafting the American River, Francis and I are on the left

We lived together for a year in his condo atop Twin Peaks with a spectacular view. I never tired of looking down Market Street to the Ferry Building, the bay, Mt. Diablo, and beyond. The view and our deck made the small one-bedroom condo seem much bigger.

When we decided to marry, we asked a mutual friend, a transpersonal psychologist, to perform the ceremony. We believed in the wisdom of the I Ching's Book of Changes written by the first Emperor of China, Qin Shi Huang (259 BC – 210 BC). The Book of Changes would give us a reading that reflected our state of mind when we asked a question, so we asked: what could we do to ensure a long happy life together? Then we threw three coins six times.

Our reading about what to anticipate in the future hinted at difficult times together. It was represented by a "ding," a three-legged bronze pot that fell over and spilled its contents. This was an ominous beginning and we wanted to throw the coins again but we only had one chance.

As wedding gifts, Francis and I asked our friends to contribute to our travel fund. We saved more money when I moved my favorite golden ring, which a friend and jeweler made for me in college, from my right hand to my left hand. Getting married was as easy as signing a legal form at City Hall.

Francis and I had enough money to take a trip and agreed we'd go to Asia. Francis's roots were in Shanghai and I was sure he'd want to go to China. But we thought we'd get to China another time so we decided on Japan. At last I was going to Asia! We soon took off for a month-long honeymoon holiday in Japan.

I was entranced with Japan and Japanese art. In grad school I had studied one of the best Japanese art collections in the country at the Cleveland Museum of Art. Ever since then, I couldn't wait to see Japan. Francis was excited to see Asia for the first time too.

On October 22, 1983, his birthday, we touched down at Narita Airport at midnight and I finally set foot in Asia!

The next day I called Mitsuo, the exchange student at my high school during our senior year, who now lived in Tokyo. In school, we had a crush on each other that grew when we were practicing our parts in "The Glass Menagerie." We even went to the prom together and after-prom parties. I never thought I'd see him again as I waved good-bye at the airport and held back my tears.

I hadn't seen him in twenty years and I wondered who he had become. On the phone, he said he'd meet us the next day. He insisted we stay at his home in the suburbs.

The next day he arrived with his wife and said they had recently gotten married too! She looked so with-it in casual clothes and Mitsuo said they had gone to Honolulu for their honeymoon. What a coincidence that we'd all recently started a new chapter in our lives.

Mitsuo drove us to his home where we met his parents, who welcomed us with hugs. It was midday but we still had jet lag so we crashed on a futon on a tatami mat with a big comforter over us. The next morning we rolled up the comforter in the middle of the room and put it in a closet, and the guest room was transformed into a family room again.

Mitsuo had become a small business owner rather than a company man. He employed eight accountants in his office, which the family had built as the fourth floor of their small house. He told us he was active in the Lions Club and had gone to many conferences in other countries. What a force he'd become.

Later that week, Mitsuo drove us to a famous shrine in the redwoods, about an hour north of Tokyo, called Nikko. We had arrived in Japan during momiji, when the leaves of the Japanese maple trees turn golden, rivaling New England's fall. The Nikko National Park was famous for the resting place of a famous ruler in the 1600s and it has the distinction as the country's most lavishly decorated shrine.

At Nikko, Mitsuo's wife announced she was pregnant. An expression of joy flashed across Mitsuo's face. I fantasized about Francis hugging me with joy if I told him I was pregnant someday.

20

The best part of our trip was in Kyoto. We explored many Zen temples, which were the opposite aesthetic of the colorful Nikko temple. Most of these small Zen temples had a rustic feel and were made of wood. Delicate paintings on paper screens of the seasons were used as movable walls. Most temples were surrounded by extensive manicured gardens with rocks half-submerged in the ground.

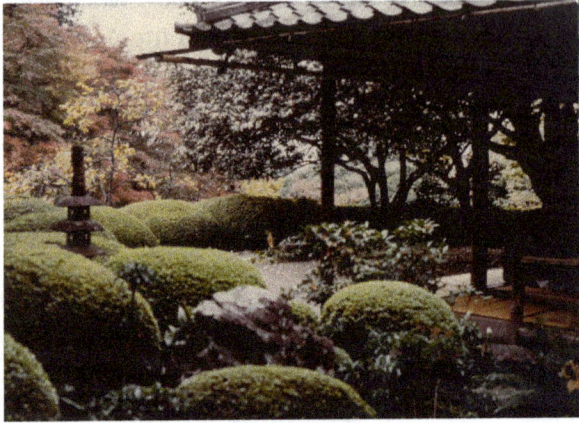

Kyoto's temples and gardens were memorable

On one excursion, we found Ryoanji (Peaceful Dragon) Temple, the famous temple with white sand rather than grass in the courtyard. There were no trees, only fifteen rocks and the garden was surrounded by low-earthen walls. I appreciated the Zen belief that having the intention to sit calmly on a pillow was where the practice began and doing this for the benefit of all sentient beings was important. We pondered the meaning of this Zen art while sitting on a bench overlooking the rock garden. These temples were the beginning of my grand tour of dozens of temples representing many faiths throughout Asia.

Before I started my adventures in Asia, I had practiced zazen at the Zen Center in San Francisco, sitting calmly on a pillow letting all thoughts and feelings pass through my mind, and having compassion for all living beings.

While living with Francis in San Francisco, I organized Coit Tower's 50th Anniversary Celebration. I brought the eight living Coit Tower artists together, then in their seventies and eighties, and showed their recent work at City Hall. I went on to organize three other large exhibits for corporate clients including one of contemporary paintings and calligraphy by artists from Hong Kong.

Francis introduced me to the editor of a weekly newspaper that served Chinatown. Soon I was covering cultural events for *East-West News* and meeting interesting people on interviews. I was fortunate to meet a famous writer and photographer for *The Sunday Times* of London, Eve Arnold, who encouraged me to visit Asia as a writer and photographer. At that time, her advice seemed like the most exciting thing I could imagine.

Besides helping me network, Francis changed my life forever when he gave me my first personal computer. Soon I was writing more and longer pieces for East Coast publications.

Frances and I had many great times river rafting, hiking, attending workshops at Esalen, and going to dinner with friends. Soon the idea of starting a family emerged, but we didn't get much further than our ambivalence. After several months of trying to decide our future together, we realized we wanted to go our separate ways. One night in bed, I noticed he was reading *How to Take a Vacation with Your Ex-wife*!

My three years with Francis were memorable. He not only gave me my first trip to Asia, but also gave me my first PC, which made me more competitive as a writer. I was ready to step out on my own to try new things, meet new people, and see exotic Asia. We parted amicably and soon I was on my way back to Asia.

Travels

In seven days I saw most of Burma (Myanmar)

I arrived in Bangkok, Thailand with a month's vacation. I was so excited to take my first trip to Asia by myself. When I stepped off the plane, I felt like I was on MARS! Everything looked so different, and It was hot and humid even in the early morning. After hours of sitting in traffic, I finally got to Gwen's apartment building.

She immediately hugged me when she saw how exhausted I was after spending almost an entire day on the plane. She took me to the nearby market for cold pineapple, mango, and papaya on sticks. I saw several monks in saffron-colored robes each holding a big bowl, begging for rice from one stall to the next. Bangkok even smelled different; the crowded market was filled with the aroma of grilled meat.

Gwen was still dynamic and a lot of fun at sixty-five. She shared her apartment with three other Peace Corps volunteers in their early twenties. She had been an AP stringer and a good friend of my parents. We met when we both lived in Washington, D.C. a few years earlier. She had married a surgeon in Ohio, but he was a workaholic, so Gwen, a striking tall blond, signed on with the Peace Corps. She consumed lots of vitamin C to stay healthy and looked very youthful.

After getting her hands dirty from manure by making methane gas stoves in the country near Chang Mai, she was assigned to Bangkok at the Department of Agriculture, the most important department in Thailand. When I met her, she was making a video about vines choking the canals and hampering trade and traffic in Bangkok.

She wanted me to know she was still ritzy and later that day took me to the polo club for a drink. Then she whisked me off to the Continental Hotel for a fantastic Thai dinner.

That night I called my friend, Jerry Burchard. He'd lived in Bangkok for ten years and had several gallery shows of his photographs in Bangkok. For about a third of the year he lived in San Francisco, teaching photography at the prestigious Art Institute.

The next day on my way to meet Jerry for lunch, I kept saying to myself, I'm in ASIA! My taxi took me past tall pointed spires on temples and the most famous temple in Bangkok with a small emerald Buddha inside.

Jerry and I met at a restaurant near his home where he treated me to a hot spicy shrimp and noodle dish that helped cool me off. Then we each took a tut-tut (a motorized rickshaw) to his apartment where he showed me his huge color photos of a place called Pagan where he had recently visited—a place with many very old temples in northwest Burma.

His photos grabbed my attention because of the specks of light in the black sky that looked mystical, with palm trees in the distance, shaking in the wind. His technique was to take a long exposure over a whole night with a large aperture, which made the scene look surreal. For several minutes I couldn't take my eyes off those mesmerizing shots.

A glimpse of Jerry's photos of Pagan

I knew I had to see Pagan. Jerry told me where to get a visa and the next day I was in Rangoon, the capital of Myanmar. Bangkok looked tame compared to Rangoon. I'd never seen a country stuck in that kind of time warp.

I arrived about dusk and my guide took me to the Shwedagon Pagoda for a full-moon festival. It seemed like a thousand people strolled around the grounds peacefully. I may have been the only white face there but inside the temple grounds it felt serene because I was surrounded by people who embraced the value of loving kindness. The temple was shaped like a golden Hershey's chocolate kiss with a tip thirty stories high.

Shwedagon Pagoda is the most sacred pagoda for the Burmese, containing relics of the Buddha. I wandered around the temple in the light of the full moon.

Very thin women and men wore sarongs or skirts that wrapped at their waist and fell to the ground. The cloth had different patterns for men and women. They seemed so cool. I was glad I'd bought cotton t-shirts and capri pants in Bangkok because I'd brought the wrong clothes from San Francisco, which were too heavy and hot.

The grounds of the 325 foot Shwedagon Golden Pagoda

The women had a pale yellow paste on their faces, a mark of beauty (and a natural sunscreen). These people were poor but they still bowed to each other as a sign of reverence. Bowing was a very old custom through most of Asia and was still followed in many places.

The Burmese believed in Theravada Buddhism, which dominated Southeast Asia (Sri Lanka, Cambodia, Laos, Thailand, and Burma). Mahayana Buddhism migrated northward along the International Silk route from India into China. Later, monks took Mahayana Buddhism to Tibet, Japan, and Korea. Buddhists world-wide subscribe to virtues such as refraining from killing, stealing, sexual misconduct, lying, and using drugs.

Pagan once had 10,000 Buddhist temples; now it has about 2,000

I spent my first night in a kind of hostel; I lay awake counting the biggest cockroaches I had ever seen crawl over the floor in the light from the bathroom. The faucet water was brown. I didn't want to stay another day in Rangoon, but I still wanted to see the rest of the country and especially Pagan.

Unfortunately, the only way to see the country was on a guided trip and all the guided trips were full. I needed three more people to make a trip possible and give me seven days to travel around the country. I was getting desperate when my driver from the night before took me to the airport to catch a plane back to Bangkok.

Fortunately, my good luck prevailed and on the only flight from Bangkok that day I met two teachers from Oakland, California, coming from Guangzhou who wanted a guided tour. Another traveler from Paris joined us, Bridget, whom I'd met at the Burmese consulate the day before. We had four passengers— enough for a trip through Burma! My confidence soared and I knew I'd see Pagan.

The cost of a week-long truck trip through Burma was a carton of Western cigarettes, and Jerry had told me to bring a carton and $40. If you didn't bring cigarettes, the trip cost $250. American cigarettes were desired but were also contraband.

Our truck driver and guide filled up several plastic containers with gas because there were no gas stations on the entire trip. I was always glad to get out of the truck for a stretch on the day-long road to Pagan. It seemed dangerous with all that gasoline sloshing around in the back taking up the little space we had.

Breathing the smell of gas for so long upset my stomach. Our driver was smoking like a fiend and throwing his cigarettes out the window. I worried it would just take one to set the gasoline ablaze.

After three hours on the road, our driver said we'd stop at a Chinese restaurant. I was hungry for fresh veggies but what arrived consisted of a few carrots in gravy with rice that tasted awful and made me sick just to look at. The owner tried to impress us with a new CD by Madonna but he had no idea what the words meant.

Madonna was singing, "Papa, don't preach. It's my baby and I'm going to keep it!"

It was a surreal moment; only a week before, I'd seen Madonna singing this song at the Live Aid Concert on TV in San Francisco. In less than a week, the footage had been duped in Singapore and sold throughout Asia. No one seemed to honor Intellectual property rights.

After lunch we were back on the road. Finally, after a day and a half, we were in Pagan, a tiny village in northwest Burma. The first thing I saw was a group of women washing their clothes in the Irrawaddy River's brown water. I had come to see the temples that the Burmese built beginning in the ninth century. These temples stretched as far as I could see. 10,000 temples had been built on the flat plain from the ninth to thirteenth century when Pagan was the capital of the Mandalay region. It was the first kingdom to unify the vast area that would constitute modern Myanmar. Now there are about 2,000 temples because many had been looted by people and destroyed by the environment.

A store on the way to Pagan

In the 12th and 13th centuries, Pagan and the Khmer Empire in Cambodia were the strongest empires in mainland Asia. The Burmese language and culture gradually became dominant in the upper Irrawaddy Valley. I was surprised to learn that this area was rich in many traditions: Buddhism, Tantric practices, Hindu beliefs and animist practices all mixed together.

The next day I was amazed to see how small the temples were. Past the river and all around me as far as I could see were small temples on the flat plain. I got this perspective from climbing up on one of the temples with the roof broken open. The vista, dotted with small clay-colored temples, was unreal, like nothing else I had seen in my travels.

The temples were mysterious, dark and cool inside except the light that came in the door or from a broken ceiling. This forgotten land seemed stuck in the past and it was a pocket of the old Asian culture that I had hoped to find in my travels.

I was also on a mission to bring a message to a craftsman. My driver asked a few people where Aung the lacquerware artist lived and I was relieved to find him so easily. Aung and I greeted each other in limited English, and I met his wife and young daughter. He showed me how he painted thin layers of lacquer on the molds and then his wife baked them in an oven deep in the ground.

As I talked to them, both parents were watching their young daughter. The entire family was reserved and very thin. I told Aung that his buyer, Dean, would be there in two or three weeks to buy more of their lovely containers. He sold them in Jogjakarta and gave Aung the profit when he returned. I'd met Dean in Bangkok at lunch with Jerry.

Aung made lacquerware in reddish-orange or dark green round and cylinder-shaped containers with images of real and imaginary animals that he painted with a brush of only a few hairs. I carried several containers home with me.

Aung showed me how he painted images of flying female spirits called Apsaras, a kind of goddess. They were similar to Apsaras painted in caves at Ajunta, which were some of the oldest paintings in India.

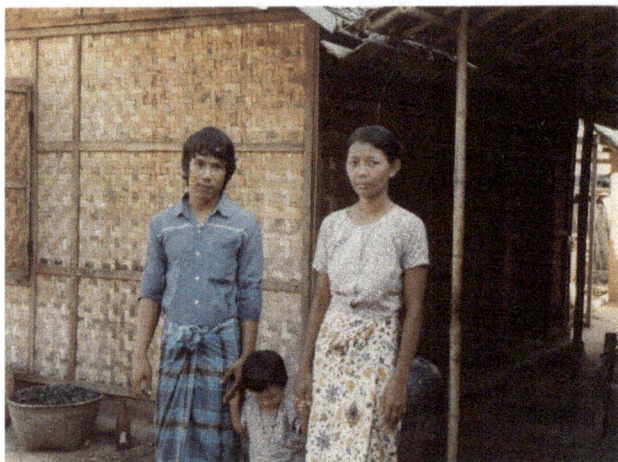

Aung and his family made lacquerware in Pagan

Our trip was almost over when we stopped for lunch. A man quickly appeared and showed us about a dozen huge beautiful rubies the size of marbles. He laid them out on the lid of a shoebox. We didn't buy any because we'd heard foreigners could go to jail if the authorities found any rubies on them.

31

The next night at Inlet Lake we stayed in a hotel. Late at night, two soldiers in uniforms with guns unlocked my door and barged into my room. They made gestures for me to get out of bed and empty my backpack. I'd been in a deep sleep and it didn't make sense. I was wearing only my panties and a t-shirt. I was scared they were going to rape me.

"Don't touch me!" I yelled. They understood.

The French woman was in tears she was so scared. I got out of bed and emptied my backpack and there was nothing there but clothes, toothbrushes, deodorant, a few bracelets and necklaces, plus an address book. When they didn't find any drugs or rubies, they left our room.

It was one of the few times on all my trips that I was really scared. The thought of being raped slid through my mind or that I might be thrown into a dark jail where people disappeared for years. I'd heard of people accused of stealing rice who were put in jail based on someone's word.

After the soldiers left, I couldn't fall asleep. The next morning I found out they'd bothered no one else and the owner of the hotel had given the soldiers the key to my room.

We went back to Rangoon on the seventh day; the last day permitted by our visa. I would have liked to have stayed much longer to see more of this country that seemed in a kind of time warp. People lived without TVs or phones but they appeared content; they had a solid faith and virtually no contact with people from the West or any part of Asia.

At the end of the trip, we exchanged our addresses like many people do after a trip. We'd had a great time keeping ourselves amused by each other's stories but I never met any of these special friends again.

I saw how the Buddhist religion dominated these people's daily life in both Thailand and Burma. It seemed to make many Burmese docile but the heat also was oppressive and the pace of life slowed down dramatically. People gained strength from their community, family, and faith, and they seemed happier living a no-tech life than many people I knew at home with every new high-tech gadget.

Tending to this spirit house brought good luck

Back in Bangkok, I was glad to see my friend Gwen. I confided that I needed a vacation from my vacation. She laughed and suggested I take a bus south to Phuket.

My week in laid-back Phuket began with a ten-hour bus ride from Bangkok. I arrived in a slight drizzle after midnight so a taxi driver took me from the bus station to a new hotel with cottages. The owner came to the desk in a sarong and I signed in. He said I could pay him the next day and hurried back to bed.

When I awoke I saw the ocean was close to my door and a small spirit house stood on a post outside my front door. Sprinkling it with water and offering fruit to the spirits every day was meant to bring me good luck. The Thais were keenly aware of the force of good luck and tried to cultivate ways to bring even more luck their way by taking care of spirit houses, daily adding fresh flowers and sprinkling water on them. Propitiating good luck was a new idea to me that I gladly took home and have come to believe in.

Bangkok's skyline of Buddhist temples

17,000 islands make up the country of Indonesia

The trip to Sumatra started in an unusual way. I was in the annual San Francisco Bay to Breakers race when a six-person, green centipede of runners from Portland ran past me and one man shouted,

"We're going to the hash harriers' 50th anniversary party next week in Kuala Lumpur!"

I was familiar with this popular running group for expats in Asia because I'd run with a group of them in San Francisco. It was known as the drinking club for people with a running problem.

I saw another opportunity to visit Asia!

At the time, I was living by myself in the Fillmore district and that night I dreamed I was in Kuala Lumpur even though I didn't know where that was. When I woke up I remembered my dream and wanted to go, but was ambivalent about this opportunity. How could I go? I didn't have the money and I had a job that I couldn't leave. But I'm resourceful and somehow I knew I would find a way to make it happen. I had the skills of a savvy journalist, a lot of bravado, and I was young and in great health.

On Monday, the day after the race, I called the editor of *Runner's World*. Usually I sent a query letter to an editor and waited for a reply that took at least three weeks. With a sense of urgency I told the editor that the event was in two weeks and I needed a letter of support saying he'd read my article on spec.

He agreed! The next day, letter in hand, I walked into the Garuda Airlines office near Union Square and told a manager I'd like airfare to Kuala Lumpur to cover the running event and that I'd mention Garuda Airlines as my carrier. He called a few days later and said I had an educational pass! I was amazed that the trip came together so easily. Garuda Airlines gave me a free ticket.

Next, I had to convince my boss to give me the time off and this was a challenge. He had misgivings, but was surprised that I'd gotten a free ticket and had a story to write when I got back. He wondered what he would do without me, but finally said he would delegate my responsibilities to others and give me a month's vacation.

Everything was in place, but I hesitated. It was a big step and I would be alone without a friend to visit. I talked it over with my good friends, Marilyn and Suzanne, whom I knew from the San Francisco Zen Center and they convinced me that I had to go.

"Of course you can do it." They said. "What an opportunity. You've been saying for a long time how much you'd like to see how ordinary people live in Asia."

Another good friend, Edie Hamlin, said, "Park your car at my house so you won't get tickets on street cleaning days. You'll be fine and I know you'll have a wonderful time."

I stayed at Edie's that night and we talked for a long time about my trip. She wanted to know where I was going so she asked me to go to her bookcase. By chance I pulled out her atlas with an inscription on the front page from Miguel Covarrubias, whom I later found out wrote the first study of Balinese culture in the early 1930s. The inscription said, "To my good friend Edie." Edie was a muralist and they became friends when Miguel painted a mural at the Ferry Building in 1937.

I could barely sleep that night; I was so excited to head out to Kuala Lumpur. That morning, I was on my way with one bag and a guide book for Malaysia. Even though I appeared cocky about my trip, underneath my bravado, I was more scared than I'd ever been. What would it be like? Would I enjoy meeting foreigners and runners from all over Asia? If I didn't like it, I couldn't just turn around and go home.

When I stepped on board that jumbo jet at San Francisco International Airport, my excitement overcame my fear. I had reached a new level of confidence by venturing forth from my familiar day-to-day routines into a vast unknown on the other side of Pacific.

From the start of my travels, amazing things happened because I was in the right place at the right time. A sense of synchronicity began to surface, which stayed with me.

Twenty-four hours after takeoff with almost no sleep, I was wired. During a refueling stop on a small island in eastern Indonesia, I met a guy on the plane who said he was on his way to Bogor on Java where he worked in a research institute. I asked him if he knew anything about the Dani people who lived at the top of the mountains in Irian Jaya. I showed him a postcard I'd picked up at the gift shop inside the small airport.

"They are some of the most primitive people on the planet," he said. On the post card, the men were wearing gourds over their penises with a string around their hips to hold up their balls. The women were wearing t-shirts and grass skirts in the photo. They looked like people I'd seen in a *National Geographic* magazine photo taken in 1910, only now the women wore t-shirts.

"If you want to go to Irian Jaya, go to Sumatra first," the researcher said. "If you like visiting a country that doesn't have many of the conveniences you take for granted, you'll manage well in Irian Jaya. These people live like they have for hundreds of years." Because of his comment, I did visit the Dani years later at the end of my travels.

Several hours later, when we arrived in Jakarta, I had to decide whether I was going to cover the running event in Kuala Lumpur for *Runner's World*, or trust my intuition and go to Sumatra. I felt

I must see Sumatra because I was sure I'd find a way to visit the Dani. After talking with several officials at the airport, I met the director of the airport and convinced him I wanted to change my destination and go to Sumatra. I had an educational pass and fortunately the director of the airport said, "I'm from Sumatra and you should see this amazing island." Synchronicity had happened again; I skipped Kuala Lumpur and went to Sumatra instead.

When I arrived, the air was muggy and I was so hot I was sweating. I was in the tropics at last. I didn't know anything about the island and wondered where to go and what I'd write about.

The next morning at 5 a.m., strange sounds blaring over a loudspeaker shocked me awake. The music came from a nearby mosque and reminded Muslims to pray. Moaning voices and music poured into the humid, black summer air. My adventures began in this enormous city called Medan, on Sumatra's northeast coast. One of the richest cities in Indonesia, Medan handles about sixty-five percent of the nation's exports, mostly crude oil.

Then I realized I couldn't take any pictures because my camera wouldn't advance. What was I going to do? After a momentary panic I thought it might need a new battery. Luckily, that's all it was.

I remembered that a monk at the Zen Center in San Francisco had told me about some of the places he had visited in Southeast Asia. He mentioned how much he'd enjoyed Lake Toba and Samosir Island many years before. I found the bus station and bought a one-way ticket. The ride was difficult; every seat taken and the bus was packed with people and clucking chickens in cages. Many windows didn't work. Several hours later, the bus driver dropped me at the ferry to Samosir Island.

When I stepped off the small boat on Samosir Island in the early evening, the market was in full swing. I heard a medicine man on a microphone talking to a large crowd of patients around him.

Good luck totems made by Bataks on Samosir Island

The dark-skinned native Bataks had a stand where they sold carvings that one man said had the power to protect me from evil spirits—that's what I needed.

I had no idea what lay ahead so I bought a foot-high carving of three small dancers standing on a wooden base with two alligators facing each other carved on the base under the dancers. I think it brought me a lot of good luck while I was traveling in North Sumatra.

I was surprised to see several boys about two years old wearing nothing. Many other slightly older boys wore shorts and a few little girls wore torn dresses. None of them wore shoes. They squatted on the dirt playing a game with marbles. While they were lost in their game, I took their picture. Although Medan is a prosperous city, the country is extremely poor and I don't think too many white women traveling on their own had passed through there.

At the market I was surprised to see two white faces in the distance and I walked over to meet them. They were doctors on vacation from Sacramento and on their way to a park with wild orangutans. They asked me if I wanted to join them. I had found my next adventure.

As we traveled through the country, I saw women balancing big baskets of food on their heads, carrying babies tucked in a material slung over their shoulders that hung at their waists, went up their backs, and tied at their shoulders. The colorful band of cloth was woven and strong enough to carry a young child. These thin women walked in a line on a narrow path through a field toward their houses. I was amazed and humbled at their strength and excited to be in their presence.

Dancers in front of their communal home

The following day we stopped to see some women in a group in front of a house with a traditional saddle-like roof almost 30-feet high. I climbed a ladder to get inside the house, which was dark and spacious. Several families lived in this communal house with the roof pointing upward so it brought them closer to the heavens.

On the front of the house were many carved and painted images of suns, stars, cockatiels, and geometric motifs in red, white, and black. The house was about three feet off the ground resting on pillars so breezes kept it cool inside.

In front of the house, several dancers moved together in a line back and forth to a drum beat. They held their hands like they were praying. I didn't know the reason for their dance but it was unlike anything I'd seen before. Women wore yellow flowers pinned to their hair and the men wore traditional red caps. The chief moved back and forth in the dance too. Because I took a lot of dance classes at home, I was fascinated by the dances in every country I visited.

One of the unusual things that I learned about the Bataks was that until about a hundred years ago they practiced cannibalism. I was a silent witness to this when I sat in a stone chair at a stone table. I had learned that the Bataks beheaded men there. This custom was widespread on many Indonesian islands until the early 20th century.

The people of North Sumatra lived close to the natural world, especially those living near rainforests and rivers. In the past, the crocodiles were feared by everyone. When they came onshore, they sometimes snatched babies while their mothers were washing clothes in the river. Finally, all the crocodiles were caught and put on a farm between Medan and the Bohorok Center. I was scared just looking at them! They were huge; some were fifteen feet long, weighed more than 300 pounds, and could outrun most people.

I saw crocodiles carved on many small wooden charms that brought good luck, I never saw an image of an orangutan and wondered why.

Red-haired orangutans in the rainforest

I found orangutans in North Sumatra's rainforest

The two doctors from Sacramento and I sped toward the orangutan center in a white air-conditioned VW. It was one of the few times I felt cool in hot and muggy Sumatra. I didn't know much about orangutans. I had never heard of the Bohorok Orangutan Rehabilitation Center at Gunung Leuser National Park, about an hour from Medan. I didn't know orangutans lived in North Sumatra and Borneo, and that they were an endangered species.

At the park, I saw a young orangutan that had been abandoned by her owners. They were cute babies but by the time orangutans were teens, they were large and difficult to manage. The abandoned orangutans had no idea how to forage for food. At the Bohorok Rehabilitation Center, they learned to find seasonal fruits and berries, and other survival skills.

A new guest house near Gunung Leuser National Park

Jeni, our guide, wearing a Save the Planet t-shirt, told us the orangutans could be extinct in twenty-five years. Orangutans only live in North Sumatra and Borneo and are endangered. The most serious threat, primarily in Borneo, was the loss of their natural rain forest habitat which was being destroyed by farmers in order to plant palm oil trees.

We wanted to see the platform where the feeding took place and got a chance that afternoon. In order to get to the center we had to cross a shallow river. When we got to the river, Jeni asked if we had our permit letter authorizing us to proceed. No one had it, and we couldn't believe we'd come this far and weren't going to see the orangutans. Since I had recently run the Bay to Breakers race in San Francisco, I volunteered to run back half a mile in the humid weather. I returned dripping wet with the permit.

When we reached the top of the small mountain about forty-five minutes later, a silence hung in the air as fifteen people squatted on the ground behind a wire fence. We arrived just in time to see one of the orangutans swing down with the greatest of ease from a fifty-foot tree to take bananas from the hand of a park ranger perched on a platform. The rangers didn't look the orangutans in the eyes because they were trying to break them of their dependency on humans.

The platform where a ranger fed the orangutans at the Center

It was amazing to see these animals so close. There were about five feet tall with reddish hairy coats and flat, black faces.

After watching the feeding for an hour, which only seemed like a few minutes, Jeni took the three of us on a four-hour hike in the rainforest. The slippery ground made it hard to walk, and the forest was dark and noisy from the sound of all the insects.

First I heard an orangutan, then I saw one standing on a tree-limb. Then another wild orangutan appeared. I was overcome with excitement that I'd seen one orangutan swing through the trees and land on the same branch next to another one. When they came together on the branch, one nibbled the other's toes. I felt like a voyeur watching what might soon become an amorous scene. Jeni recognized Mina, a five-year-old who had been released from the Center three years before and was mating with a much larger male, about ten years old.

This experience overwhelmed me! I've never forgotten it. It's a tragedy that these beautiful animals are almost extinct. Jeni conveyed the plight of the orangutans and he managed to gain donations to help them survive.

"The rainforest is incredibly rare and beautiful," he said. "Only eight percent of the earth's land is covered with rainforest, which supports half of the planet's species. As lush as it is, however, the rainforest's ecosystem is extremely delicate and must be managed carefully as an invaluable world resource."

Like Jeni, I wanted to linger in this wilderness.

Jeni explained that orangutans share nearly ninety-seven percent of their genetic material with humans. Our close genetic relation with all the great apes makes us cousin species. Their arms stretch out longer than their bodies, over seven feet from fingertip to fingertip. Like humans, orangutans have opposable thumbs and big toes.

For the first year of its life, a young orangutan holds tight to the mother's body as she moves through the forest in search of seasonal fruit. The next year, the youngster follows the mother as she moves through the trees. After the second year, the young are on their own.

Playful young orangutans swinging in the trees
Photo courtesy of Oran Utan Republic Foundation

Jeni's vast knowledge about the ecosystem as well as orangutans impressed me. We became friends and the next day we went rafting in inner tubes down the Bohorok River.

It reminded me of running the rapids on the north fork of the American River in California's gold country, but this water was warm and easy going.

I felt a growing attraction to Jeni. He was about five-feet, six-inches with a slight frame, big dark brown eyes, and dark skin. Like me, Jeni was also divorced and we were both glad to find a new interesting friend. He'd been a guide at the park for many years after graduating in biology from a university in Medan. We began to find out more about each other over lunch at an outdoor restaurant that served spicy fried rice with veggies.

Then, like a date at home, we went to a movie, *Dog Days*, about vicious German Shepherds killing cops in a small Texas town. This silly movie was made for export but Jeni said many of his friends believed America was like that.

Many years later, thinking about my incredible adventures in eight countries—including five islands in Indonesia—I realized this trip was one of the most memorable. Meeting the orangutans in a North Sumatra rainforest was a thrilling experience. I was becoming a risk-taker and getting better at trusting my intuition. At that time I didn't know I was going to write about this trip and that I was destined to return to Asia.

Chance meeting in Bali

Never in my dreams did I think I would ever set foot in Bali, just south of the equator. When I arrived there, I thought it was the most exotic place on the planet. One of my inspirations for coming to Bali was Margaret Mead. I saw her when she came to my university to speak about her biography, *Blackberry Winter*. I remember at the time that I wanted to see Southeast Asia especially Bali and twenty years later I was there.

Balinese practiced witchcraft with elaborate ceremonies for cremations and they had ways to lure ghosts to their ancestor's home. Several times I heard musicians played hypnotic gamelan ensemble music. The blend of gongs, xylophones, drums, bamboo flutes, and plucked string instruments was a strange ethereal sound. The musicians sat on the right side of the stage about six feet from the stage, which was only three feet off the ground.

I also saw the puppet theater which used only light and shadow. The puppets, crafted from buffalo hide, were mounted on bamboo sticks that the puppeteer held up behind a piece of white cloth. With an electric bulb or an oil lamp as the light source shadows were cast on the cloth screen. The stories were well-known to the Balinese and were based on Indian epics, the Mahabharata and the Ramayana.

In the 1920s and 30s, Bali inspired many artists. They made the three-month trip by steamer from New York to this Dutch colony. When the steamer arrived on the north shore of Bali, the weary travelers were rowed to shore in small boats.

I was coming from the airport sitting in an open-air truck that was a cheap taxi for up to six people. When you arrived at your destination, you said, "stop," and the driver told you the fare. Sometimes riders bartered down the price. This cheap means of travel is still used throughout Indonesia.

When I arrived, my eyes took in everything about my surroundings. As the driver was speeding down a narrow road with two lanes of traffic, only an hour after I'd arrived, I was still telling myself, BALI, I MADE IT!

Many people were walking alongside the road since they walked everywhere close to their homes. I did a double-take when I saw the back of a medium-size woman with long auburn hair. I knew only one woman like that.

When the truck was a few yards away, I yelled, "BONNIE!" She turned around and when I saw that it was Bonnie, I yelled, "STOP!" and the driver came to screeching halt. I got out of the back of the truck. I was excited to see her and find another woman from San Francisco traveling by herself. We hugged each other with joy. If I had passed by a few minutes later, I might not have seen her.

She told me where she was staying near Ubud, the cultural center of the island, and I rented a room in a house close by. Many tourists lived with a family so they saw the intimate daily rituals of women sprinkling water on shrines, putting fresh flowers in small vases and bowing to sacred places in their home and courtyard. Together Bonnie and I explored Ubud and nearby Peliatan.

One afternoon we met at a café overlooking a small pond with pink lilies. The air was hot and humid so a cold mango drink tasted good. I asked Bonnie about her travels, where she had been and whether she was planning to stay in Bali for a while. She'd been living there for a month. She told me she had seen the most amazing sight—orangutans in North Sumatra's rainforest! We'd both been at the tiny center that cared for orangutans— almost at the same time.

If I hadn't seen her, she would never have known I was there. Later in San Francisco, looking at her photos, I was overcome with memories of the orangutans I saw swinging in the trees, coming down to the platform where they were fed until they could find food themselves. In all my travels, seeing these orangutans was the most thrilling experience.

Bonnie had a good rapport with the editor, Don George, of the travel section of the *San Francisco Examiner* and she took her photos to show him. He was so impressed with her shots of these gentle red-haired apes that he wanted to print them almost immediately. Usually it took months to get an editor to read an article and if it was accepted, several more months to see it in print. The editor needed a travel feature to accompany Bonnie's photos.

Bonnie came to me and asked if I could write the travel article. A travel piece wasn't like a journalistic story: I would have to weave my impressions into factual material and interviews. My story's themes would be about the orangutans and life in the village near the park. I wrote the story and focused on the fact that this entire species could disappear in thirty years without major interventions to save them. I explained how different life was in this area where most people were Muslims, and how I had become friends with my guide and we went tubing down the Bohorok River.

Was I surprised when my story and Bonnie's photos filled the entire front page of the *Examiner* travel section, one of the most prestigious travel sections of a major daily newspaper. In a side-bar, "How to Get There," I mentioned Garuda Airlines as my carrier and their terrific service on such a long flight to Dempensar Airport on Bali. This coverage met my end of the obligation for an educational pass.

I sent a clip of this published article with every subsequent query. It gave editors a sense of my expertise to write about Asia. Tourism officers knew I'd come back with a fascinating story. Just like that, I became a travel writer.

Within six months after my trip to Sumatra, the Malaysian Tourism Department invited me to visit! I joined nine other travel writers from the Bay Area, who flew first class to Kuala Lumpur, the capital of Malaysia.

But I'm getting ahead of myself. Let me tell you about my adventures in Bali and the Hungry Ghost festival.

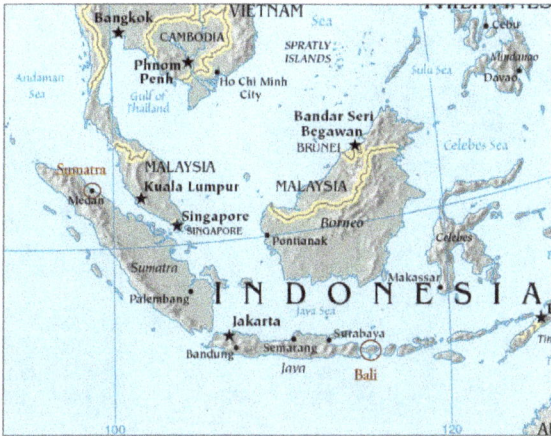

Bali is one of the most fascinating islands in the world

I wanted to see a place where everyday life has rituals, processions, temple festivals, or commemorations of some kind. The Balinese live close to the spirits and natural powers that surround them. I wondered if this might be a kind of utopia, a version of Shangri-La.

In the Balinese universe, everyone is endowed with magic energy called "sakti," which a person accumulates. Some people are born with a greater amount of this energy and they become the priests and witch doctors. They are trained to serve through the art of magic.

Daily, someone sweeps the stone floors in most homes and sprinkles water on holy places to honor the spirits. Most of the people are Hindu without the emphasis on cycles of rebirth and reincarnation. Many also follow Buddhist traditions and believe in local and ancestral spirits.

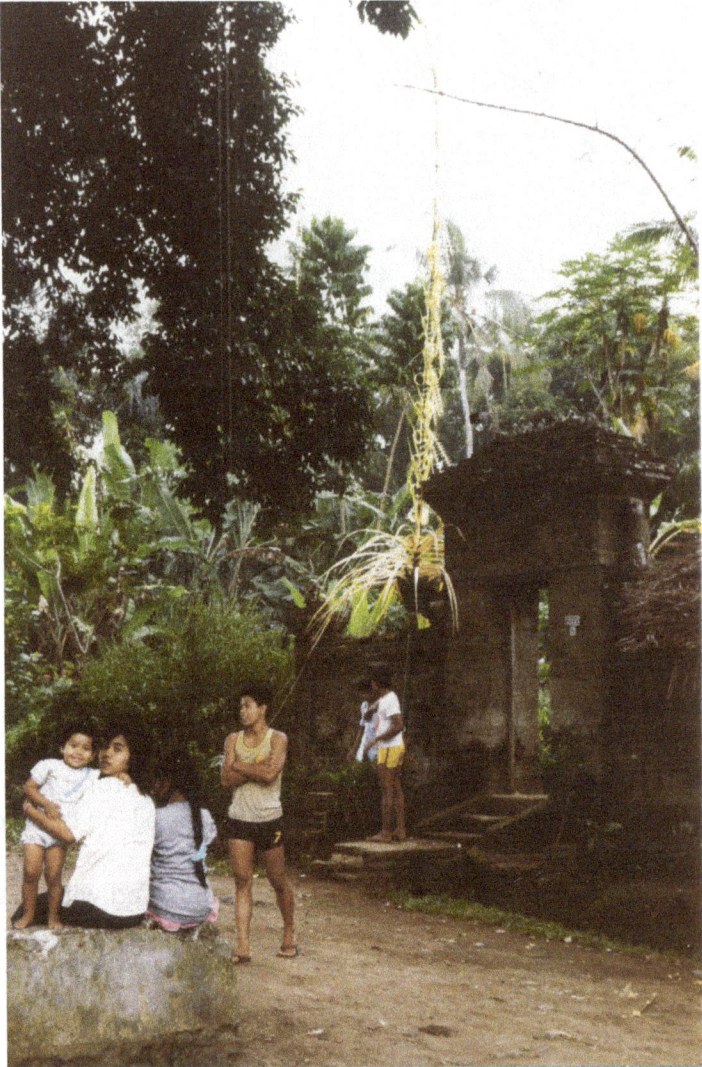

Families made long bamboo poles (penyors) with carvings

Synchronicity played a big part of my trip to Bali. By chance, I arrived on the first day of the Galungan festival, when hungry ghosts came back to visit their ancestors. The Balinese make bamboo polls thirty feet that hang above homes. They put food offerings on roadside shrines and in their homes for the ghosts.

I made my way to Pelitan, the cultural center of the island where I met a painter who sold traditional paintings in his gallery, like one of his ancestors, that included ghosts and demons.

Arsa gave me this drawing of his ancestors

I struck up a conversation with the artist, J. Wayan Arsa, and he invited me to his home in back of the gallery to meet his wife and two sons. He invited me back the next day to make dozens of small offerings stacked on plates that were placed in the family shrines behind their home.

I made offerings of food for the hungry ancestors

The offerings would make the ghosts happy for their annual visit with their relatives. While walking around after spending time with the artist and his family I tried to cool off in the heat and humidity at midday. Later on my own I was drinking mango juice at an open air table near the side of the road to Peliatan when a dark-skinned man about ten years younger than me pulled up on his motorcycle. He ordered a cool drink and asked if he could sit at my table. He introduced himself as Wayan Sidhakarya and told me he was a writer.

He wanted to tell me how this festival was celebrated in homes and in the community. He answered most of my questions and then presented me with a typed manuscript several pages long about the Galungan festival. I was surprised he gave it to me.

"Galungan, a major cycle of feasts, is celebrated as the time when the gods and deified ancestors return, and therefore the evil spirits have to first be appeased so they don't disturb the ceremony." Wayan explained.

"Families strengthen their devotion to their ancestors by making cakes for offerings. The day is celebrated with new clothes, and families worship in their temples at home and entertain themselves with performances or other enjoyable activities.

At the end of the celebration, ten days after it began, people go to Tirta Empul Temple at Tampak Siring Spring to pray and bathe, for the spring water has a curative power."

The Galungan festival includes a long procession

The market at Ubud, Bali

After we finished our juices, Wayan wanted to show me the Tirta Temple and baths about twenty minutes away. I got on the back of his motorcycle and we arrived as several Balinese were bathing, wearing sarongs in the water. I walked over to the bath made of stone and walked down the steps into the warm water in my clothes. The feeling was wondrous. In the heat I quickly dried off as we whizzed down the road to see the forest of monkeys.

Close to the Monkey Forest, I bought a chain of ten monkeys holding on to each other's tails. The stand where I bought them had a painting with little boxes for each day; this was a beautiful calendar with two dragons facing each other and an image of Shiva as the Lord of Dance, in the middle. The owner hated to part with it but sold it to me after explaining he need money to buy his family new clothes and presents.

The day after Galungan, families relaxed, because they had given offerings and prayers to their ancestors.

A Balinese goddess has many attributes of Hindu goddesses

A carving I saw of a Balinese dancer looked like an Indian dancer with her body tilted at the waist. This dancer resembled one of the paintings of Apsaras at the Ajanta caves, dating from 200 BCE. Apsaras are heavenly singers and dancers. I hoped to find some trance dancers like the ones I'd seen in a film that Margaret Mead made in the 1930s. The film showed men in a temple dancing in an ecstatic frenzied way, communicating with the spirits. They pressed sharp knives against their chest and you'd think they would have become mortally wounded but they weren't harmed while in a trance.

I saw one of the sacred dances, the Lelong dance of virgins, performed by four young girls. This dance was originally performed in a temple. At the age of four, girls are chosen from the community to learn to move their eyes, fingers, hands, face, tiny bodies, and feet in complicated positions that take years to perfect. For performances, the girls wore ornate costumes. By fourteen they were considered too old for this temple dance.

The famous Lelong dance of virgins

My week in Bali was almost mystical. It seemed like everyone I met was a writer, dancer, jewelry maker, mask maker, or someone with creative talent. These people had such reverence for the spiritual world. I wanted to stay and see more festivals but I was glad I was able to see the beginning of the Hungry Ghosts festival. Rites and rituals for each festival had to be honored. I wanted to stay longer, but I had to get back to work.

The Mother Goddess festival is celebrated throughout India

I believe synchronicity propelled me to a profound experience in India. My trip began in New York when I was on business and I stopped to visit two friends who imported goddess figurines from Greece. We met a friend for lunch who had recently finished writing a book about the goddess celebrations in India. The next festival was in October, the Mother Goddess festival. This festival influences every aspect of a Hindu's life and the Mother Goddess empowers Hindus to make changes in their lives. This festival is celebrated all over India.

In India, the Mother Goddess is the symbol of the earth's fertility. World-wide she is worshiped under many names and similar figures have been known in every part of the world, some from the earliest known history. She is represented as the creative force in all nature, the mother of all things, and is responsible for the periodic renewal of life.

Inspired by my recent involvement in earth-based rituals, I wanted to participate in India's Mother Goddess festival, something I had never heard of. The festival includes Navratri, a nine-day long celebration when Hindus venerate the Mother Goddess in all her manifestations. Dussehra is the tenth day of the celebration when the force of good overcomes evil.

At that time, I had just reviewed a large exhibit of Indian art at the Asian Art Museum, "The Essence of Indian Art." The exhibit included a fabulous collection of artwork from the earliest time in India to the present. *East-West News*, the newspaper where I was on staff, devoted a page to the story.

I sent my review of Indian art to the Indian Consulate in Los Angeles hoping to get a press tour. When I was given a phone interview, I persuaded the director of the cultural affairs office to send me to see the Mother Goddess festival six months later. I was excited to see this festival in Kullu, in the Himalayas, but the director arranged for a trip during the Great Goddess festival that included Chennai, Bangalore, Agra, Delhi and ended with the last day of the festival in the Kullu Valley of Himalayas.

My first destination, Chennai, a huge city on the coast of the Indian Ocean, was my first glimpse of India—twenty years after my graduate courses. I was met at the airport by a friendly woman who said she would show me how the festival was celebrated there. A car drove us through the congested, noisy, hectic city, smoggy from too many cars and motor bikes. Most people were walking and bicycling. The sight was a feast for my eyes—so many different colored saris that women wore from their head to ankles.

The beggars I associate with India were also there and it was sad to see such misery. Also, there were many Hindu and Buddhist temples and monks in saffron robes with serene smiles.

Although I hoped to see India by train and be closer to the way most people lived, I was hosted by the tourism office like a wealthy American and stayed in the best hotels. There were dancers one night, music and drama at other stops. I was whisked around in a car by a chauffeur, a surreal experience considering the ways most Indians traveled.

From Chennai in southern India to the snow-capped Himalayas, traditions of goddess worship are celebrated that began 2,500 years ago. This was the time the Indus Valley civilization thrived in the cities of Mohenjo-daro and Harappa, now in Pakistan.

The Mother Goddess has several representations. As Durga the warrior, she is celebrated for killing the buffalo demon after the male gods failed to destroy him. She is also venerated as Parvati, the voluptuous consort of Shiva, the god of destruction or rejuvenation. She is also incarnated as Lakshmi, goddess of wealth and prosperity.

During Dussehra, the last day of the Mother Goddess festival, Indians celebrate the triumph of good over evil as explained in the epic poem, the Ramayana, which recounts the story of how Prince Rama and his lovely bride, Sita, left their kingdom to make their way in the world. Sita and Rama symbolize the archetypal lovers.

The legend tells how Sita is abducted by a hideous ten-headed demon named Ravana. Sita then uses all her worldly charms and seductive beauty to distract the demon long enough for Rama, who has an army of monkeys and bears, to attack and kill him. By vanquishing these and other life-threatening perils—both psychological and worldly—Rama and Sita are hailed as triumphant heroes when they return home from their arduous journey.

Every night during the festival, dramas of Rama and Sita's victory over the demons are performed on outdoor stages in villages and cities throughout India. On the last night of the festival in Agra, I watched as colorful 20-foot high papier-mâché effigies of Ravana and his two brothers were set ablaze to trigger a fusillade of firecrackers. This finale symbolized the belief that the force of good reigns supreme.

In Agra, where the Taj Mahal is located in central India, I stood in a huge crowd while a woman dressed as Sita was paraded through the crowd on the back of a convertible like a beauty queen. Dressed in a golden sari draped in garlands of pink jasmine, she waved to the crowd as she passed by. An army of men costumed as monkeys and bears scurried around her to protect her from demons. Marching bands and children streamed along the crowds.

The Mother Goddess festival honors the warrior goddess Durga
Photo courtesy of Wikipedia

To celebrate the warrior goddess, Durga, the residents of Mysore in southern India start the festival with a dramatic elephant procession. In the traditional manner of the Sikhs (warrior caste), the procession is led by a man dressed like a raja, seated on an elephant, in front of a hundred elephants decorated with glittering tassels. Huge brass trumpets blare and the pounding of war drums fills the air, as men dressed as soldiers in ceremonial uniforms and nobles in traditional costumes march past.

The festival is also venerated in the workplace. When I visited Bangalore, India's "tech center," I was lucky to get an interview with the vice president of the prestigious Tata Company, a conglomerate that includes the U.S. equivalent of Apple, plus a steel company, an auto manufacturer and more. After the interview, the vice president invited me into the conference room for the employees' celebration of the festival.

Much to my surprise, a swami blessed all the company's computers, placing yellow flowers on each terminal and sprinkling them with holy water. The Tata vice president told me that Navratri is a time when Indians bless the objects that make their work possible.

I joined software designers and secretaries in the conference room as the swami placed coconuts, incense, and candles on a makeshift altar and then sprinkled each of us with holy water. We ate small delicious cakes before returning to our work.

I was also privileged to experience an intimate view of how the festival is celebrated in the home when my guide and her neighbor invited my friend and me to join their celebration. My guide apologized that she hadn't prepared her family's shrine.

Nevertheless, her attention to daily ritual amazed me. While raising a family and working as a tour guide, she still found time to let the "sleep goddess" out the back door as her first ritual of the day. Most mornings my guide also made intricate geometric designs with colored chalk on the sidewalk in front of her suburban home.

At her neighbor's home, a seven-tiered shrine dominated their small living room. Covered with painted miniature statures of Durga, musicians, dancers, monkeys, bears, lions, and many other ornaments, these ten-foot tall shrines are displayed only during the festival.

One night, while on my way to the home of a young man from the India Tourism Office, I saw a group of five children walking down the street carrying candles and small brightly colored papier-mâché dolls.

The children's ritual marks the end of Dussehra and the beginning of the marriage season. This is regarded as an auspicious time to consummate a marriage, since nine months later the mild weather helps to ensure a newborn's survival.

After Dussehra comes to an end throughout most of India, the small Himalayan village of Kullu begins its own seven-day celebration, one of the most spectacular in the entire country. More than one hundred goddesses and gods from temples in distant valleys are carried into this "valley of the gods."

The festival cannot begin until the powerful goddess Hamibda, guardian of the festival arrives from Manali further up the valley. Many statues of Hamibda and other divinities are pulled through the narrow streets on wagons. Other divinities are carried on platforms that rest on the shoulders of two men. Villagers line the streets watching the procession pass.

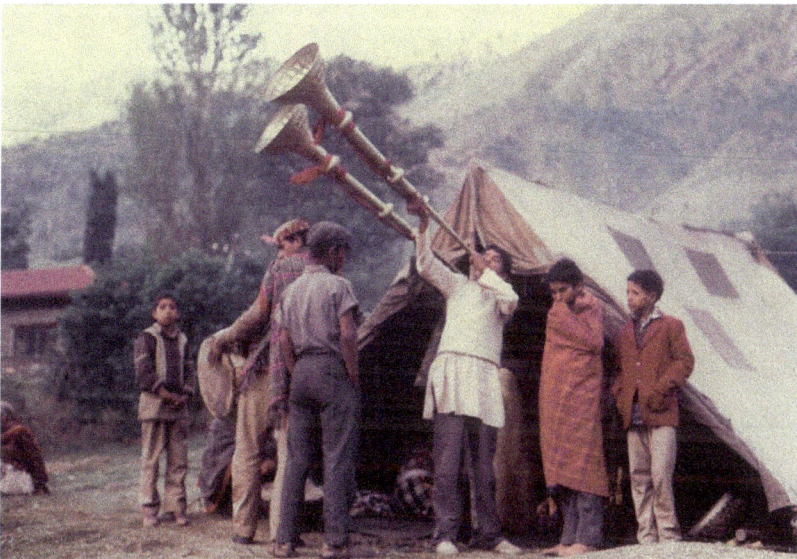

Horns announce the arrival of the goddess Hamibda in Kullu

Marching into town, men beat drums and blow fifteen-foot brass horns. In the background, viewers can see small wooden houses stacked in precarious tiers on the sides of the formidable mountains that flank the valley.

Long into the night, villagers maintain vigils at the shrines, which are housed in tents dotting the valley. The sound of hypnotic ragas pulsates through the cool air while thousands of yogis,

Tibetans, Shikhs, and other Hindus bargain with the vendors for used clothes or a new refrigerator.

One tiny shop I stumbled upon was filled with ripe orange persimmons that lined the dark walls. Two short women with long black hair sold fruit and paintings of gods and goddesses. Elsewhere, men, women, and children dressed in colorful cottons filed through a large tent to view photos commemorating the 100th birthday of Jawaharlal Nehru, the first Prime Minister of India.

A shop in Kullu sold persimmons and paintings of Durga

I wandered past a canopy decorated with tinsel and lights and inhaled the aromas of fresh hot popcorn and incense. Vendors sold delicious, saffron-colored sweets and tasty curry dinners. I bought a few of the distinctive knitted hats, gloves, and slippers in wild neon colors, which women make during the long winters.

Shops were clustered together according to the items for sale, and their wares were sold at the same prices—an unusual show of cooperation in honor of the Mother Goddess.

This gathering is generally the last opportunity for residents of far-flung Himalayan villages to meet before the winter snows isolate them until the following spring.

A family in Kullu celebrating the Mother Goddess festival

I saw children dressed like Rama and Sita dancing on a small open-air stage. One man dressed like a monkey, complete with a long tail, wandered through the town. He symbolized one of the monkeys and bears who rescued Sita from the demon so she could be reunited with her husband, Rama.

I was sad to see a handicapped man dressed in bizarre clothes with a garishly painted face roll past me on a wheeled board, unable to sit up while he begged for donations.

A man dressed as a monkey in Rama's army

In the bustling market, children played computer games and wandered about the rides and exotic animals that attracted thousands of visitors every day. I roamed the streets with two Parisian filmmakers and a painter who had recently been painting in Srinagar.

One afternoon I hitched a ride on a motorcycle and zigzagged through dense traffic to a temple about fifteen minutes from town. Carved out of the face of the mountain, the temple was set off with broad stone steps rising from the wide river that flows into the valley.

After climbing five flights of steps, I got down on my hands and knees to crawl into a dark cave that held a statue of the Mother Goddess. At the end of the small chamber, the statue was almost completely covered with fragrant garlands of yellow flowers. In the flickering light of candles, only the goddess's head showed above the flowers, like an infant's head crowning at birth.

Many times my memories of this trip filled me with wonder. I felt a deep connection with the Mother Goddess and silently gave thanks for this powerful experience on my personal pilgrimage.

Whirlwind trip in China

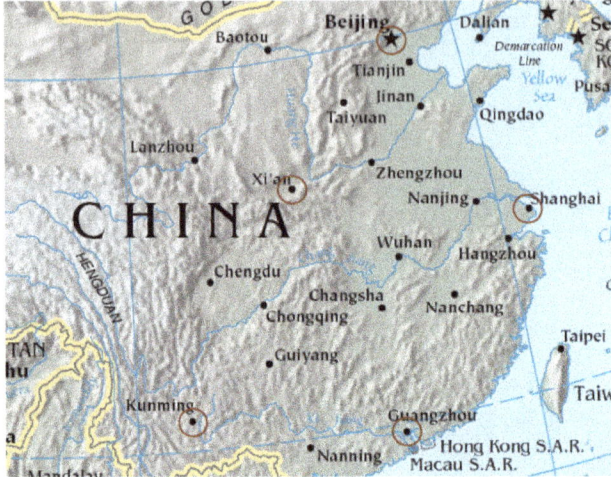

China has fascinated me since I was a teenager

I'd written for *East-West News*, a bilingual weekly newspaper in San Francisco, for six years before my trip to the Peoples Republic of China (PRC). This paper began as a way to keep city officials and Chinese Americans aware of what was happening during the Cultural Revolution.

I'd recently reviewed an enormous exhibit, "Treasures from the Shanghai Art Museum: 6,000 years of Chinese art" at the Asian Art Museum of San Francisco. The Department of Cultural Affairs sent some of China's best classical art for the exhibit. It was the first of many cultural exchanges between sister cities.

In 1988, I worked with the Chinese tourism agency on a trip to Bejing, Xi'an, Kunming, Guangzhou, and Shanghai. I invited Bonnie Kamin, a photographer and friend to join me. The Chinese treated us as though we wrote for the *Washington Post*. It was easy to host us in the middle of winter when only a few tourists visited.

Chou, our guide, Bonnie, me and three journalists in Xi'an

In Beijing, the first thing you see is the terrible pollution from burning coal for heat. The air quality was terrible. Our tour guide, Chou, met us at the airport and whisked us off to the National Tourism Office. The first thing we did was walk on the Great Wall and later saw a very small high tech area.

From Beijing we flew across the immense country to Xi'an on the western border and the terminus of the International Silk route. I wanted to see The Museum of Qin Terracotta Warriors and Horses, located roughly 25 miles east of Xi'an, where archeologists had unearthed about 2,000 of the 8,000 warriors.

This massive archeological discovery includes life-size terracotta soldiers, wooden chariots with horses and cavalry horses, officials, acrobats, strongmen, and musicians.

The first emperor, Qin Shi Huang (259 BC - 210 BC), is known for his two great achievements, the Great Wall and the Terracotta Warriors and Horses. He had a profound influence on Chinese history and culture by implementing a standard written script of ideograms. He also devised the I Ching Book of Changes used for forecasting the future, which I used in my wedding ceremony to forecast what my husband and I needed to have a loving, successful marriage.

**The Terracotta Army of 8,000 warriors is a World Heritage Site
(From a postcard of the Terracotta Army)**

I had a fascination with Xi'an since I learned it was one end of the Silk Road. Extending 4,000 miles, the Silk Road is named for the lucrative Chinese trade carried out along its length. It began more than 2,000 years ago. Trade on the Silk Road was a significant factor in the development of the civilizations of China, the Indian subcontinent, Persia, Europe, and Arabia.

A second archeological discovery unearthed the Famen Temple and some of the finest art from the Middle East. Famen Temple was built in the 15th century on a plot of land that had been a place of worship since the 3rd century. This temple was originally a stupa—memorial mound that housed relics of Shakyamuni, the historical Buddha.

After an earthquake in 1981 toppled the octagonal 13-story brick pagoda, archaeologists discovered a secret chamber hidden beneath a stone slab filled with hundreds of glass, ceramic, gold, silver, and bronze objects.

Archeologists made a huge discovery at Famen near Xi'an

From the dig, the archeologists learned that glass imported from the Middle East was considered a luxurious art form. The plates and bowls unearthed were imports from Arab countries, and showed the designs of early Islamic glassmaking.

My last stop in Xi'an was a visit to a film studio where four women producers told Bonnie and me about their next project, *The First Emperor of China,* a co-production with the Canadian Film Board. The following year I saw this fantastic film with hundreds of actors at the IMAX theater in San Francisco. Before I left on this trip I'd seen one of their best films, *Red Sorghum,* an unforgettable story of courage by the Chinese, and ruthless conquest and cruelty by the Japanese during WWII.

After visiting Xi'an, Bonnie and I went to Kunming, near Vietnam's border where we met the Li, who are part of the PRC's one-percent of the minority population. A fair was underway when we arrived and I laughed at kids riding on a zebra that really was a dark horse painted with white stripes.

Our final destination was Shanghai, the most modern city in the PRC, which was undergoing tremendous construction. I was surprised to see a small stock exchange, a room with a few tables and chairs. Only in Shanghai did women wore stylish clothes.

On my short list of things to do in Shanghai was visit a hospital where Qigong, an ancient medical practice, was used. At the clinic I almost fell out of my chair when I saw a doctor step into a circle of patients and begin to turn around inside the circle, and then step back and take a Tai chi pose as he projected his healing energy from his fingers into several sick patients. He moved back and forth, projecting his chi as he went around the circle again. This method appeared to be effective and many very sick people went home well. The patients also practiced Qigong exercises during the day.

The next day we went to the Temple of Heaven, a huge round building with three roofs in consecutively smaller layers until they reached a golden round ornament at the very top. We had to go up ten flights of steps just to get to the first floor. We came very early so I could see others practice Qigong at 6:30 a.m. to stay healthy. No one wore a hat, gloves, or even a coat; they were very hot from the exercise as I could see from their red faces.

China's cultural reach was enormous in Asia since Chinese settled all over Asia, taking their customs with them. The country I saw was in the midst of a gigantic leap forward forty years after it had become a republic. The Chinese had survived the Cultural Revolution and later Western ways influenced people living on the eastern coast and in the countryside.

High on Ko Samui

Ko Samui is a tiny tropical island east of Phuket

On one of my trips to Asia, I met a handsome guy who matched my interest in Asian adventures. Christian Jaulin was smart and handsome, a French geneticist doing research at the Pasteur Institute in Paris. His dad had been a pilot for Air France so his family members gained a benefit of free travel to anywhere Air France flew. He preferred to take his annual vacations in Southeast Asia and usually stopped at a place called Peace Bungalows on the island of Ko Samui.

We met scuba diving at the Bunaken National Park Dive Centers in Monado, Sulawesi, one of Indonesia's 17,000 islands. Both of us had come to see one of the world's best underwater parks.

In the park, the coral reef was teeming with colorful fish. We were in the Celebes Sea Large Marine Ecosystem. This part of Indonesia is located southwest of the Philippines and is characterized by a tropical climate with sparkling clear, warm water.

This was my first time scuba diving and I had never seen so many fish, from tiny gold striped fish to larger green fish a foot long, and many others even larger. Few places in the world compare to it.

I told the driver of the boat I could swim well and wanted to do a dive. I was amazed he let me dive without any lessons! I put on an oxygen tank, a mask and fins and was ready to go.

He said, "Breath like you do here and you'll be fine!"

I sat on the side of the boat and leaned backward like the other experienced divers had done. For a few moments I was scared—the ocean was so vast and I might get water in my mask.

I started swimming toward a diver in the distance and made gestures I wanted to join him and another woman swimming with him. I felt much safer then and we saw dozens and dozen of fish, of all shapes and sizes. The variety of color and shape of the corals was amazing too.

Christian and I had a great time diving. Also, we both liked the friendly people in Indonesia who seemed more relaxed than in any other country; maybe because the equator went through it and the heat made people more languid.

With other divers from Hong Kong to Belize and other places, we had carefree days of dives and dinners, and sat around a picnic table talking long into the muggy nights. We decided to travel together to the next destination, Rantepao on the west coast.

From Manado, we flew south to the capital, Makassar, and caught a bus that took us through spectacular terraced rice fields on the sides of mountains. Eight hours later we finally arrived in Rantepao, where many funerals are held. While many tourists find their funeral customs gruesome, the Tourism Department thinks they draw many tourists annually and have not stopped this integral part of their culture.

We arrived at an auspicious time when a king was about to be buried. It had taken the family and village several years to organize the funeral. The ceremony involved a priest ritually slaughtering twenty-four water buffalo in front of the villagers and tourists. With a single stroke of a huge knife the leader of the village cut the jugular vein of each bull and it fell to the ground. A few men carried it to the side as another bull was brought forth. By the tenth dead bull Christian and I were physically sick. It was terrible to watch. Neither of us could believe this was still their custom, which probably began hundreds of years ago.

On our last day together in the mountains, Christian told me he was going to a place called Ko Samui and invited me to meet him there. He took out a map from his backpack and showed me the island of Ko Samui, southeast of Bangkok in the Ardamen Sea.

When Christian and I met up at Peace Bungalows on Ko Samui, I was overcome with tears—I was so happy to see him again and he was so sexy in bed. I was smitten with him and the intensity of our friendship grew over the next week.

The air was hot and heavy at Peace Bungalows and the owner who greeted me was a short smiling woman in a sarong. She was glad Christian had come back another year. We were unbelievably happy during that week together. We lounged in the sun day after day. I lost track of time—swimming, tanning to a deep brown, smoking weed, and eating the best Thai food only a few feet from the ocean's edge.

Our bungalow was about 10 feet from the ocean

A restaurant we visited for brunch was owned by his friends who had left Paris many years ago. Christian asked for a special omelet that had THC in the butter so the omelet gave me a buzz.

Christian and I fell madly in love in Ko Samui

One night a huge storm struck and we closed our wooden shutters as fast as we could. We both had a hit of Ecstasy and I lit a candle. It was hot but we snuggled close together under a sheet. We were so glad to be with each other and shared more about our lives that night. Our friendship grew even more intense. In the three weeks since we met at the dive center, we had learned so much about each other.

He proposed that I move to Paris! I wondered how I could I live in Paris and communicate with my terrible accent and do my work. I might feel isolated but I'd pick up the French with my personal tutor and eventually we'd get married. This was the first time that I had felt love at first sight, and the ecstasy of our love and the drug made us feel even closer.

I had gone to Ko Samui for a vacation and when I left I thought I had fallen in love. Christian had an exotic appeal, a mystique since he lived so far away in a glamorous city. He was one of the most interesting guys I'd met and he cared a lot about me. I wanted to go! Was this going to be the next phase of my life as a wife, a mother, and a writer?

A month later, Christian came to San Francisco for two weeks and it seemed like we were back in Ko Samui. But by that time,

I had called the writer of the guide book I used in Indonesia. I discovered he lived in Oakland on the other side of the Bay from San Francisco.

Of course, he enjoyed the flattery when I called and he asked if we might have dinner the following week. We had a lot in common besides our many trips in Asia.

Soon we were seeing a lot of each other and I liked his two teenage daughters. He didn't mind that Christian was coming to visit for two weeks. I was glad he was so reasonable and my relationship deepened with both men.

After interviewing for a post-doc position at UCSF in genetics, Christian and I became tourists in the city. I had a great time hanging out with him and one of our most memorable adventures was rafting with friends on the American River.

This was the only time I had intimate friendships with two men. By the end of the next two weeks, I told Christian I wasn't coming back with him to Paris. Soon after this, Bill decided to return to Big Sur since he missed his kids and wanted to live close to them.

I always had projects, writing, work, and good friends but I suddenly found myself sad that both men had gone in different directions. It hit me hard about six months later and I needed help to rise above my sadness of these lost relationships. Fortunately, soon I was leading a tour to Cambodia and Vietnam.

Discovering Angkor Wat in Cambodia

Angkor Wat is a the biggest temple in Asia

Soon after both Vietnam and Cambodia allowed tourists to visit in the early 1990s, they attracted adventurous well-to-do visitors. I was asked to lead a tour in 1993 sponsored by HoliAsia Tours in San Francisco. Our group arrived In Phnom Penh, the capital of Cambodia, and the five of us caught a small prop-plane to a village, Siem Reap, about ten miles south of Angkor Wat, the capital city of Siem Reap Providence in northwestern Cambodia. When I disembarked, a rainbow appeared overhead and I took it as a good omen for a place I'd find most memorable.

This girl's family lived outside of the temple

I was so excited to see this famous and enormous ruin since the woman who shared a flat with me in the Castro district of San Francisco had gone there to help people adjust to losing a limb due to buried land mines. As a physical therapist she sent me letters with many grueling descriptions of her experiences. We were both members of a group the was dedicated to prevent the return of the Khmer Rouge. From 1975 to 1979, they were responsible for the Cambodian genocide where upwards of two million people lost their lives.

The height of the Khmer power in Asia was from the eighth to the fifteenth century. Angkor Wat was built by the Khmer King Suryavarman II in the 12th century.

From a distance, the temple looked like a mountain in the center with four smaller temples at each corner. The inside of the temple was full of Buddhist and Hindu images as well as reliefs of devatas, female nature spirits. Discovering so many female images was a tremendous surprise.

The Khmers had been visiting the ruin long before Westerners arrived. This temple was buried in the dense tropical jungle when the French naturalist, Henri Mouhot, wrote about the ruin in 1886.

Part of Angkor Wat emerged from the forest

Angkor Wat grew until the surrounding land couldn't provide enough water for the thousands who lived there. Finally, the once bustling city disappeared in the jungle.

The United Nations declared Angkor Wat a World Heritage Site in 1992. When my group visited in 1993, a crew of Indian archeologists was restoring the monument. Unfortunately, the looting in the temples was terrible. I was furious that so many Buddha heads had been lopped off from the statues by thieves. The sacred heads, now just objets d'art, devoid of their original meaning, were taken to Bangkok, crated, and sold to buyers worldwide.

At Angkor Wat, our guide, Kim, took us to the most famous and unusual temples as we toured the enormous grounds in two small jeeps. We trekked up and down stairs in the cool mornings and Kim gave us details about the temples. We were accompanied by guards with rifles to protect us from the Khmer Rouge.

Dancing divinities, Apsaras, adorned the walls of many temples

On many walks in the jungle, I met kids in t-shirts and shorts and others in sarongs. They were trying to sell almost anything to tourists including musical instruments. It was hard to pass them without making a purchase, knowing that even a little money would help them improve their lives.

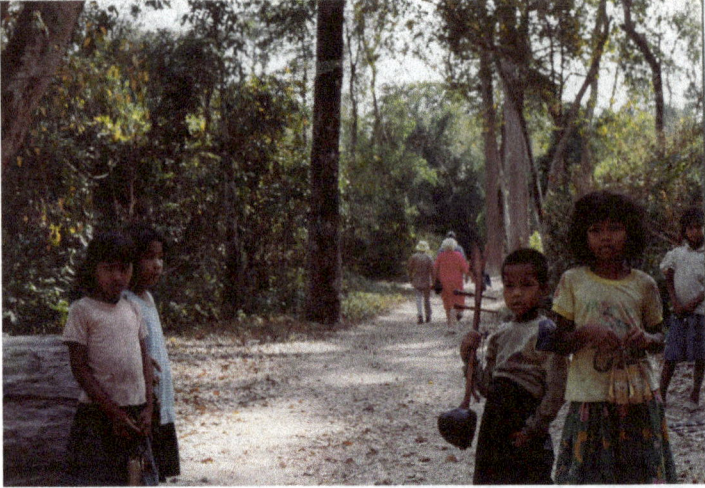

Kids playing at Angkor Wat and selling musical instruments

One night at dinner, an angry employee rushed into the hotel dining room waving a pistol and shooting in the air. I was terrified and ran into the kitchen, my chest pounding. Others ducked under the table. No one was hurt and eventually someone talked him into a calmer state. He was furious that he'd lost his job there since there were so few jobs. This hotel, the only one in Siem Reap at the time, was built during the French colonial times. It was old and dilapidated, with brown running water in the bathroom.

Twenty-five years ago when I first visited, Angkor Wat was just becoming known to tourists world-wide. It was hard to believe that a decade later it would be flooded with tourists and many modern hotels.

My tour began in Halong Bay and ended in Saigon

Besides Cambodia, the new and exotic place for seasoned travelers in 1993 was Vietnam. A few of my friends were living in Hanoi and several more were trying to get entrepreneurial businesses off the ground despite the many regulations enforced in the socialist country. One woman published a magazine about Vietnamese culture and another wrote the first guidebook about Vietnam.

After watching the Vietnam War on TV for so many years, I felt like I was the enemy when we first arrived in Hanoi. But within a few minutes my feelings changed. I liked the Vietnamese from the start—they were so friendly and seemed as curious about us as we were of them. During the fifteen years after the American War, as they called it, the population had doubled and there was no animosity toward Americans.

Hanoi was full of stately cream-colored French villas with dark green shutters that gave the city a charming feeling, a bit like New Orleans. We stopped at many famous places, including Restored Swords Lake in the middle of the old city where a friend of mine lived. Later, Barbara and I got together for tea so I could find out what was really going on there.

A busy market in Hanoi

She said they celebrated many festivals in traditional ways like people did before the war. The Viet Cong general, General Giap, had often been the honorary official at these festivals. The war was a distant memory even for those who fought.

Life was much better for most people though some families were still coping with the after effects of war. For instance, Agent Orange, the chemical weapon used to defoliate the jungle, had left many children physically and mentally maimed even though it was four generations since the war ended. Also where this chemical was used the land was unable to grow rice. Agent Orange also affected American soldiers causing a number of neurological problems.

Traditional weddings were still popular in the 1990s

In Da Nang, a large city on the coast about midway between Hanoi and Saigon, I arrived in time to see a wedding. The bride and the other women attending wore traditional ao dai. This dress with a long split almost to the waist reached their mid-calf. They wore white pants underneath that reached almost to the ground. The bride had just stepped inside the house where the ceremony was going to take place. This family's life seemed to embrace old traditions. Several years later I heard from a friend living in Saigon that white wedding dresses from the West filled the front windows of many stores.

On the last night, actors staged an impromptu opera that was a gesture of friendship. It was a warm night and we sat outside on chairs as others in the community took seats. The actors were dressed in elaborate costumes and the opera had fantastic sets, even a small orchestra. It was a wonderful surprise.

Saigon, our last stop, was their L.A.—crowded, smelly, dirty, exciting, and vibrant, like no other city in Vietnam. You could easily be killed walking across any boulevard since there were so many bicyclists and motorcyclists but almost no cars or stop lights.

Our guide took me to the Women's Tour Company (WTC) that had contracted with HoliAsia, the tour company in San Francisco that sponsored the trip. We had guides in all the cities we visited and a friendly guide went with us on the entire trip. In Saigon, the WTC headquarters was in a French colonial mansion that once housed the headquarters for the American military. I walked through the building that General Westmoreland had used as his headquarters.

As another gesture of friendship, my guide and the head of the agency insisted I have my photo taken with them. I liked most of the Vietnamese I met, they were friendly and wanted to meet Americans who had come so far to discover their country. I knew that soon Vietnam would soon become an international tourist center, and I was glad to have visited when the people were still close to their old traditions.

Grass skirts and penis gourds

Indonesia's 17,000 islands include Irian Jaya in New Guinea

In a *National Geographic* magazine from the late 1920s that I'd bought for a quarter at a sidewalk sale, I read about and saw photos of some of the most primitive people on the planet, the Dani, who lived in the central highlands of western New Guinea called the Baliem Valley. They were discovered on an expedition in 1926 by the Smithsonian Institution and Dutch Colonial Government.

I'd vowed at the beginning of my travels that I would see the Dani, and finally I had the chance. Through an acquaintance I found out about Nico B. Pasaka, a successful entrepreneur who owned a tour company for the eastern half of Indonesia. I called him in Sulawesi and asked if he would help me meet the Dani in Irian Jaya. He said yes. I was astounded at my luck and flew to Jayapura, the capital of Irian Jaya, and took a small prop plane to a mountaintop airport in the Baliem Valley.

Was I surprised when I landed! The men staged a dance for tourists, jumping up and down with long spears. They're known for their two-day victory dance after an enemy is killed. They take weapons and ornaments from the enemy during battle and use them in their dance.

Dani tribesman like the ones I saw in 1993
Photo courtesy of Wikipedia

These men and women had dark skin, fuzzy black hair, and were about five and a half feet tall. The once bare-breasted women now wore t-shirts and grass skirts, and the men wore a gourd over their penis that was tied around their waist. They were even more exotic than I had imagined.

I arrived just in the time for the yam harvest. Men dug up the yams from the ground and a group of women cooked them in a big pot over an open fire. When it was time to eat lunch, I sat between two dark women about my size on the ground shoulder to shoulder. We were so close I could smell them. It was an indescribable odor. All ten of us were as one shape sitting with our legs stretched before us in a comfortable position on the ground. Lots of kids ran around in shorts.

I was excited to be with these women—curious about their life—yet felt we lived on different planets. I couldn't believe I was having lunch with the Dani on a warm summer day. The yams were bland and filling. After we ate on plates with spoons we relaxed and the women talked among themselves.

They were friendly and touched my long golden blond hair. We communicated primarily with pidgin English and laughter as I touched their frizzy black hair.

I was glad I'd brought my Sony camcorder to record these unusual people. I began to shoot footage of a man in shorts and a t-shirt with a sad expression telling me in his version of English how precarious the life of his fellow tribesmen was on the mountaintop. He had earned a teaching certificate but couldn't find work in Jayapura so he returned to his tribe. He wanted to teach the kids in his tribe but didn't have pencils or paper. He wondered out loud, "How can they survive in the world I've seen in Jayapura or will they remain as they ever had?"

He added that medical care was poor, and many people died by forty from tuberculosis and lung-related problems from breathing in so much smoke in their tents.

That afternoon, I took my Sony camcorder to the market in the center of the village. I couldn't wait to buy a grass skirt! I tried on several of the long grass skirts that tied at the waist and one was just right. I had to have a penis gourd as a souvenir. A sign at the market advertised fax service—an unexpected convenience.

On the third night, it started to rain. The mountain air was cold and someone motioned me to come into a small tent. About ten Dani men and women sat around the small fire for warmth. We sat shoulder to shoulder and I felt safe and warm. I enjoyed hearing the unusual sounds in their language. A few spoke pidgin English. They were talking very fast. When one of them turned on some music they began singing, "We care for our mother earth, she is our mother."

My Shangri-La

Thirty years ago just about anything Asian excited me. I had an overwhelming passion to see Asia. At times, I saw myself as a kind of cultural anthropologist like Margaret Mead and a reporter on deadline for *The Washington Post*.

When I got to Asia, I traveled to areas that fascinated me like the Mother Goddess festival in India. My trip to Pagan in Myanmar was a lark and I had no idea what I was getting into. It turned out to be an intriguing adventure and more dangerous than I could have imagined. I wondered if I'd make it out of the country alive!

At times, my excitement was almost beyond words, such as arriving by chance on the first day of the Hungry Ghost Festival in Bali. This festival encourages the ghosts of ancestors to come home for a feast. I was also entranced to see orangutans in the wild in the rain forest of North Sumatra.

On another island in Indonesia, Sulawesi, I convinced the tour guides to let me do a dive, although I'd never dived before. I was amazed at huge colorful fish and corals. This was also where I met my friend from Paris, Christian, who knew a lot about Asia too. Later, I was overwhelmed at the contrast between the pristine natural beauty of the rainforest and the sea and Jakarta the biggest, dirtiest, chaotic business hub in Indonesia.

One of the most interesting aspects of my travel was seeing how people expressed their religious beliefs. I saw more temples than you can imagine, spirit houses, and ancestor shrines. Many temples were remote and difficult to get to. For instance, Angkor Wat, the biggest temple in Asia, had just opened to tourists. It was almost impossible to see Pagan. It was much easier to see temples influenced by Zen beliefs in Kyoto.

Upon reflection, I realized basic differences between the Asian way of life and mine. In the U.S., it seems most anyone through hard work and education can become a success. Our lives are about the opportunities we have and the choices we make. In

Asia, the most you could hope for was a steady government job, and few people had access to any education.

While many rice farmers with small incomes had few expenses, it never occurred to them that buying things would make them happier. They knew little about a market-driven economy. Local business was based on bartering and payoffs. In many countries, there was no separation of church and state, and religious beliefs created a strong sense of national identity.

Most Asians were limited as to what they could do by family and religious traditions. State policies determined how business was done. Political dissent didn't exist in most countries, and military coups often toppled governments. Some countries were still ruled by a succession of kings. In Burma, people feared their government. If a man was suspected of stealing rice, he was thrown into prison.

In every country, women worked hard raising a family and taking care of domestic chores. Some also made lacquerware, carvings and batik sarongs. Women also found time to look appealing. The idea of beauty was determined by where you lived. In Burma, for instance, women wore yellow paste on their pale brown faces, and in Kullu they pierced their nose and wore heavy silver necklaces.

You may wonder why I stopped making these trips. I realized I'd never fit in. Families and businesses were dominated by men. Most women stayed at home and raised many children. Their lives revolved around this kind of social structure. Since I didn't speak any Asian languages, I always depended on a translator to understand what was said. And I wanted to live in San Francisco, not Saigon.

Asia continues to be an important part of my life. When Vietnam became more open, I led a tour, helped open a showroom in Saigon, raised funds for a medical clinic in Da Nang, and wrote articles about the arts and business for magazines and newspapers. I have friends who live in Saigon, Tokyo, and Sydney. At home, I still enjoy visiting the Asian Art Museum of San Francisco, their special exhibits like "Yoga," and their outstanding permanent collection. I have fond memories of the place where

I got my start writing about Asian art.

My many trips to Asia showed me that chance and intuition were as important as making plans. Often I went to places I'd never heard about and found experiences that I'd never imagined. My confidence in making new friends made it easy to find allies in my travels. I found many places of "old Asia" before they were developed and deluged with international tourists. This was one of the most exciting times of my life, and I'll never forget the adventures I had to bring you these stories.

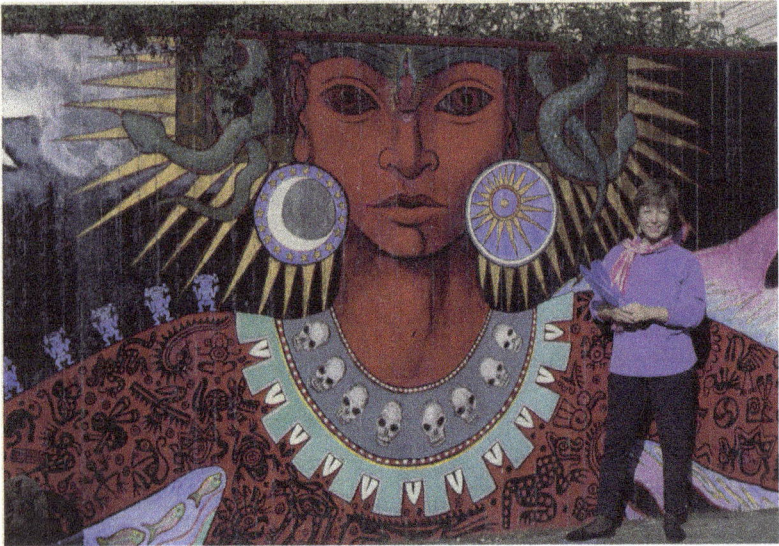

Sally back home in San Francisco's Castro district

One more thing

Publication Credits

Selected articles published on Asia
Artweek, cover feature, May 1980
San Francisco Examiner Travel Section, cover feature, Nov. 1988
Art & Antiques
The Christian Science Monitor
Discovery (Cathay Pacific's in-flight magazine)
East-West News (1983 to 1988)
Going Places (Malaysia Air's in-flight magazine, cover feature)
New York City Tribune
The Oakland Tribune
San Francisco Focus
TravelAge (West, Midwest)
Vietnam Today
Yoga Journal

Previously published book on Asia
Dove Dances Through Asia

Illustration credits
All of the maps in this book are from the Wikipedia Asia and Southeast Asia entries.

All of the photos, unless noted, were taken by the author.

Travel today to destinations in *My Shangri-La*

Travel agents offer tourists valuable information on flights, hotels, and transportation. They can customize a tour or direct you to the best package. Asia is an exciting place to visit; you can explore some of the largest cities in the world, or discover traditional festivals, environmental wonders, and sacred sites. With all the incentives to visit, you may be surprised to learn that only seven percent of travelers from the US went to Asia in 2012.

For your convenience, I've listed the embassies and consulates for more current information about the countries I visited.

1. Cambodia
The Royal Embassy of Cambodia
4530 16th Street NW
Washington, D.C. 20011
Monday to Friday 9:00 a.m. - 12:00 p.m, 2:00 p.m. - 5:00 p.m.
(202) 726-7742 ext. 13

2. India
Indian Embassy
2107 Massachusetts Ave NW
Washington, D.C. 20008
(202) 939-7000 and (202) 775-5200

Consulate in San Francisco: 415-668-0683

3. Indonesia
Indonesian Embassy
2020 Massachusetts Ave. N.W.
Washington, D.C. 20036
(202) 775-5200

4. Republic of Myanmar
Embassy of Myanmar
2300 S. Street, NW
Washington, D.C. 20008
(202) 332-3344

5. The People's Republic of China (PRC)
Embassy of the PRC
3500 Williamsburg Lane, NW
Washington, D.C. 20008
(202) 495-2266   Monday 9:00 a.m. - 6:00 p.m.
Visa office is open Monday to Friday, 9:00 a.m. - 2:30 p.m.

Consulate in San Francisco
1450 Laguna Street, San Francisco, CA 94115
(415) 674-2900
Consulates in L.A., Houston, and New York

6. Thailand
Royal Thai Embassy
1024 Wisconsin Ave NW
Washington, D.C. 20007
(202) 944-3600

7. Socialist Republic of Vietnam
Embassy of Vietnam
1233 20th Street, NW Suite 400
Washington, D.C. 20036
Monday to Friday: 10:00 a.m. - 5:00 p.m. EST

Consulate in San Francisco
1700 California Street
San Francisco, CA 94109
(415) 922-1707

www.ingramcontent.com/pod-product-compliance
Lightning Source LLC
Chambersburg PA
CBHW060951040426
42445CB00011B/1104